Annette Wolter

African Gray Parrots

Purchase, Acclimation, Care, Diet, Diseases
With a Special Chapter on Understanding the African
Gray Parrot

With Color Photos by Outstanding Animal Photographers
and Drawings by Fritz W. Köhler

Translated from the German by Rita and Robert Kimber

American Advisory Editor: Matthew M. Vriends, Ph.D.

BARRON'S

First English language edition published in 1987
by Barron's Educational Series, Inc.
© 1986 by Grafe und Unzer GmbH, Munich,
West Germany
The title of the German book is *Der Graupapagei*
All rights reserved.

All inquiries should be addressed to:
Barron's Educational Series, Inc.
250 Wireless Boulevard
Hauppauge, New York 11788

International Standard Book No. 0-8120-3773-1
Library of Congress Catalog Card No. 86-28689

**Library of Congress Cataloging-in-Publication
Data**
Wolter, Annette.
    African gray parrots.
    Translation of: Der Graupapagei.
    Bibliography: p. 61
    Includes index.
    1. African gray parrot.   I. Title.
SF473.P3W6513   1987   636.6'865   86-28689
ISBN 0-8120-3773-1

Printed in Hong Kong

456   490   13 12 11

The color photos on the covers show:
Front cover: An African Gray Parrot.
Inside front cover: Child with a tame African Gray
Parrot.
Inside back cover: African Gray Parrot and
Yellow-fronted Amazon.
Back cover: Above: African Gray Parrot checking
out a branch with its tongue before starting to
nibble.
Below, left: Bird holding a grape in its "hand"
while eating it.
Below, right: Chewing on the toenails is a gesture
of embarrassment.

Photo credits:
Hammel: pages 28 (below) and 47 (above);
Reinhard: pages ll and 38; Skogstad: front cover,
inside front cover, back cover (above); Wothe:
Pages 9, 28 (above, left and right), 37, 47 (below),
48, inside back cover, back cover (below, left and
right).

Annette Wolter is an expert on birds who has
kept small and large parrots for over thirty years.
She is also the author of two of the most popular
books in Barron's pet series: *Parakeets* and *The
New Parakeet Handbook*. From her own extensive
experience with parrots of all kinds and from
the letters of her many readers, Ms. Wolter has
learned what care parrots need and what parrot
owners most want to know. Communication with
veterinarians, scientists of animal behavior, and
breeders of parrots keeps her up-to-date on all
aspects of aviculture.

Contents

Contents

Preface

I've had Moses, my African Gray Parrot, for many years. His friendly and amusing manner, his intelligence, and his talent for whistling never lose their charm for me. When he wants to get my attention he starts a regular concert, whistling all the tunes he knows over and over again until I start playing with him or petting him. I'm only too glad to give in to his demands for affection. When I first got Moses I often used to wonder if he would ever turn into a tame and trusting parrot. For two years he flew away with loud screeching whenever I approached him with a treat in my hand. It was only after this period of time that I was allowed to pet him.

Your parrot may well get used to you more quickly; but you have to be prepared for adjustment difficulties because most African Gray Parrots arrive at their new owners' homes more or less petrified from the shock of being captured, transported, and kept in quarantine. Remain patient, and never let up on your efforts to gain your bird's affection. In this book I describe how to win and — just as important — how to keep your parrot's trust and friendship. I also discuss what an important role proper care and living conditions play in this.

Only an African Gray Parrot that receives plenty of attention, has things to keep occupied with, and gets enough exercise will stay emotionally healthy and happy. Specific suggestions for housing in a cage or aviary and for setting up a climbing tree, advice on supplying a varied diet, and many suggestions for playing with and entertaining your parrot will help you satisfy the basic needs of your African Gray.

Most owners of African Gray Parrots hope that their birds will learn to talk. Please don't set your sights too high in this respect. Not every African Gray Parrot learns to repeat words, let alone whole sentences. Many never accomplish more than whistling; some only imitate various sounds they hear; and others produce nothing beyond their own innate calls. The stunning talkers one often hears about are very rare. With the help of the tips on teaching in this book — which I along with many other owners of African Gray Parrots have tested — you can encourage your parrot's talent for mimicry, but you cannot force it in any specific direction.

The pleasures of sharing life with an African Gray Parrot are not restricted to the bird's talent for talking but derive much more from observing the animal's innate ways of expression: body language, vocal utterances, and general behavior. In the special chapter "Understanding African Gray Parrots," many patterns of behavior that you can watch every day are described. You can learn to recognize your African Gray Parrot's moods, appreciate its impressive feats of intelligence, and find out what traits are especially characteristic. Many hours of conversation with specialists in animal behavior and with experienced breeders of African Grays have confirmed my own observations and expanded my knowledge of the behavior of African Gray Parrots.

I hope that you will soon share the enthusiasm of many aviculturists for African Gray Parrots and will find that your particular bird is not only a lovable creature and a marvel of intelligence but is also endowed with a personality that is a source of pleasure every day.

Annette Wolter

Acknowledgments

The author and the publisher would like to thank everyone who has had a share in the making of this book: the animal photographers, especially Karin Skogstad and Konrad Wothe, for their outstanding color photos which depict characteristic behavior patterns of African Gray Parrots, and the illustrator, Fritz W. Köhler, for his excellent drawings. Special thanks are due to the veterinarian Dr. Gabriele Wiesner for her professional advice in preparing the chapter "Diseases and How to Keep Your Parrot Healthy."

Considerations Before You Buy

An African Gray Parrot as a Pet

I fully understand the desire to keep an African Gray Parrot as a pet and the wish to live close to this intelligent individualist, to watch the bird, and to win its trust. I know from my own experience how much pleasure an African Gray brings into a home. But at the same time I feel obliged to point out some problems that can arise from living with an African Gray Parrot.

Let us for the moment set aside the question of your personal habits and lifestyle and start with how and where you live. How will your neighbors respond to the often powerful vocal expression an African Gray Parrot gives to its pleasure in being alive? During its first few months in captivity, an African Gray Parrot is likely to vocalize its moods in screeching tones reminiscent of the jungle. Later, when the bird has adapted its vocal repertoire more to its new surroundings, its utterances will recall the jungle less often, but now it may whistle or mimic words in a penetrating voice and with a persistance that is just as grating on human nerves. Many parrots have had to leave their human families because neighbors complained about the noise and threatened legal action.

The African Gray's intelligence and personality, as well as its impressive talent for imitating sounds, whistles, and human speech, have made it so popular that it is the most frequently kept large parrot. But don't take for granted that your African Gray Parrot will be a brilliant talker. It may decide to whistle the way a dog barks, or it may like the sound of the ringing telephone and imitate it. It is best not to have any specific expectations at all, because each African Gray develops somewhat differently. What your bird turns into depends partly on its earlier experiences with people (see page 22) and partly on your patience, sensitivity, and willingness to spend time with it.

Keep in mind that the African Gray Parrot is one of the most intelligent birds we know. If an African Gray is not to languish emotionally and intellectually, it needs lots of affection, freedom of movement, enough opportunity to keep occupied, and regular company with a person it knows and trusts. Frequent and long hours of being left alone — perhaps combined with restriction of movement in a cage — are harmful for parrots. Loneliness can make these birds sick; it may trigger aggressive reactions or cause them to pluck their own feathers. An African Gray should be included in the family and be allowed to be part of family life.

Does an African Gray Parrot Fit in with Your Way of Life?

If you want to do justice to an African Gray Parrot's needs, you should answer all the following questions in the affirmative.
● If you often spend several hours away from home, is there another person around at least part of the time who is willing to pay attention to the bird?
● Do you have enough patience to get through the period of adjustment, which may last for several months, without getting discouraged?
● Will you be able to accept it if the parrot becomes more attached to another family

member than to you? (This is a distinct possibility because African Grays don't follow predictable criteria in bestowing their affection.)

● Can you keep your equanimity if your parrot leaves droppings here and there and damages wallpaper, furniture, and upholstery in your living room and perhaps in other rooms as well? (It is possible to minimize dirt and damage, but you cannot prevent them altogether.)

● Are you prepared to give over more space to the bird than the cage and its immediate surroundings?

● Would you be willing to buy or build a climbing tree out of natural branches (see page 20)?

● Do you know what you are going to do with the bird when you go on vacation or if you should have to go to the hospital?

● If you live alone, is there a person nearby to whom you would entrust your apartment key in case you should be prevented from coming home?

● An African Gray needs conscientious care and a varied diet to stay healthy. Are you willing to spend both the time and money to provide these?

● Have you considered that a parrot may occasionally need treatment by an avian veterinarian and medications and that this medical care takes time and costs money?

A healthy African Gray Parrot can live as long as eighty years! You are responsible for the creature's well-being. A separation from you and from familiar surroundings would be painful for the bird and might affect it negatively. The next owner might find it a disappointing pet, and it might end up being passed from one owner to the next. Are you prepared, therefore, to plan ahead so that if a parting becomes inevitable, your parrot will move to people who love animals and who are willing to give your pet proper care and take full responsibility for it?

Children and African Gray Parrots

School-age children quickly learn to keep a respectful distance from parrots if they have once been bitten by a bird that was overly fearful or that gave them a little pinch in a rambunctious moment. But parrots sometimes seem particularly to like being fed and petted by children, probably because of the children's small size. Babies and very small children, however, should never be left alone with a parrot without adult supervision. A sudden move on the child's part may startle the bird and cause it to bite or hack. But an African Gray that is fully adjusted usually comes to regard the children of its family as members of the flock, though they are of minor importance in the social hierarchy as perceived by the bird. All the African Grays I know have chosen an adult as their favorite companion.

An African Gray Parrot preening itself. A parrot exhibits amazing flexibility of the neck when cleaning its plumage; in order to smooth out the tail feathers, the head has to turn almost 180 degrees. Except for the head and neck, all parts of the body are reached.

Considerations Before You Buy

You should tell your children everything you know about the peculiarities and habits of African Gray Parrots and call their attention to your bird's behavior and reactions. Only in this way will they accept the bird as a family member, share in the general sense of responsibility for it, and be willing to take its needs into account.

An African Gray Parrot and Other Pets

Dog and parrot: A truly obedient dog will, if taught properly, understand and respect that the new member of the household is absolutely taboo. At first, supervision is essential because a dog barking at the parrot with front paws resting against the cage grating is to be avoided. Such an experience can destroy whatever trust the still shy and insecure bird has built up in its new surroundings and cause it to panic. The dog has to be kept at a distance. Later on, the African Gray Parrot will approach the dog on its own, and eventually dogs and parrots usually become good friends.

Cat and parrot: This is a problematical situation. Many cats control themselves beautifully and give rein to their hunting

instincts only outside. But as a rule you have to go on the assumption that a cat will attack and can wound an African Gray seriously. Keeping a bird and a cat in the same household is a dangerous experiment — unless you get a young kitten and teach it how to behave with the parrot.

Parakeets and parrots: This may be a workable combination — though veterinarians advise against it, having seen some gory results.

Two parrots: If you have bought two African Grays that already know each other and get along, there is no problem whatsoever. But if you already have a bird and now wish to get a second one of the same species or some other large parrot, the peace of the house may be shattered by quarrels and screeching, and one bird may eventually bully the other. You have to watch carefully to see if the birds are likely to accept each other or if they can't stand each other. If the latter is the case, peace will not be restored until the newcomer leaves again. So introduce a second bird for a trial period at first and make sure there are plenty of corners for both birds to escape to. The parrots will need time to get used to each other. They should never be left together without supervision, and at first it is a good idea to house the new one in a separate cage. If two parrots are confined to the same cage they can do each other serious harm.

Small furred animals and a parrot: It is not advisable to keep an African Gray in the same room with small furred animals (hamsters, guinea pigs, rabbits). A parrot flying free in the room can inflict painful wounds on small mammals.

Portrait of an African Gray Parrot at ease. The slightly raised neck and throat feathers show that the bird feels comfortable.

11

Considerations Before You Buy

What to Do with Your Bird during Vacation

It would be best if the bird could stay in its familiar surroundings and be looked after by some conscientious person. If you don't

An African Gray Parrot is very adept with its toes, using them to grasp and hold things (see inset in drawing); it eats fruit and nuts holding them in its "hand" just as we do.

know anyone who can do this, you might try putting a small ad in your local newspaper or tacking up a note on the bulletin board of your church, a local school or university, or at a housing complex for the elderly. If you are unable to find anyone, you might be able to take your parrot to someone who has experience with pet birds, to your avian veterinarian, or to the pet dealer who sold you the bird. But remember that if your bird is used to moving about freely in your home and now has to spend weeks confined to its cage, this adds to the emotional burden of separation from you. Whether or not it makes sense to take a parrot along on vacation depends on how you travel, how long the trip is, how your host or the hotel where you plan to stay feels about pets, import regulations in the case of trips abroad, and, of course, on how you plan to spend your vacation time. Being left alone in a hotel room or camper or tent would be worse for the parrot than being left in good hands at a pet store. If you want to take your bird along, this will undoubtedly affect your vacation plans because you have to figure in your bird's needs as much as your own.

Buying and Housing a Parrot

A Parrot from the Wild or from a Breeder?

Unfortunately, African Gray Parrots still reproduce so rarely in captivity that most of our pet birds have to be imported from Africa. Pet dealers primarily offer parrots caught in the wild. Domestically raised parrots are usually obtained from breeders, though occasionally they are available at pet stores.

Imported African Gray Parrots

As man has changed the natural world in Africa to make the land useful to his purposes, African Grays have lost much of their original habitat there. Thus a flock of wild African Gray Parrots has become a rare sight. Since June 6, 1981, the African Gray Parrot is a protected species under the Convention on International Trade in Endangered Species of Wild Fauna and Flora (CITES) and may be caught and exported only with special permission.

Catching African Gray Parrots is not as simple as you might think. Some biologists and ethologists who have worked in an area where African Gray Parrots live and hoped to learn more about these birds have realized with disappointment that as mere observers without special equipment they were unable to gain much insight. African Gray Parrots lead a quiet and unobtrusive life in tall, densely leafed treetops. Only in the morning and evening is a flock occasionally seen flitting by very fast and calling loudly. The natives know where African Grays breed and probably the specific trees where they nest. When the nestlings are a certain age, bird catchers climb up in the tall trees and shoo them out of their nests. Once the birds are caught, they are taken to collection points from where they are packed into special transport crates and shipped, primarily by air, to their countries of destination. Anyone who has to deal professionally with these frightened, wildly biting birds wears thick leather gloves as protection against their sharp beaks. No wonder that an African Gray Parrot from the wild will for the rest of its life associate leather gloves with the rough handling it experienced when it was caught and will for some time get frantic whenever it sees someone with leather gloves approaching.

Even when the parrots arrive in their new homelands, their trials are not over. In accordance with the law, they have to spend at least 30 days in a U.S. Department of Agriculture Animal and Plant Health Inspection Service (APHIS) quarantine station under veterinary supervision. During quarantine, pet birds are kept in individually controlled isolation cages to prevent any infection from spreading. Psittacine or hook-billed bires are identified with a leg band. They are fed feed medicated with potent antibiotics, as required by the U.S. Public Health Service, to prevent psittacosis, a flulike disease transmissible to humans (see page 46). Food and water are readily available to the birds. Young, immature birds needing daily hand-feeding cannot be accepted because removing them from the isolation cage for feeding would interrupt the 30-day quarantine. During the quarantine APHIS veterinarians test the birds to make certain they are free of any communicable disease of poultry. Infected birds will be refused entry; at the owner's option they will either be returned to the country of origin (at the owner's expense) or humanely destroyed.

To reserve quarantine space for your bird, write to the port veterinarian at the city where you'll be arriving and request Form 17-23. Return to the same address the completed form, together with a check or money order for $40 (persons planning to import pet birds should first contact the veterinarian in charge of the import facility for current costs) made payable to USDA. The balance of the fee will be due before the bird is released from quarantine. The correct address is:

> Port Veterinarian
> Animal and Plant Health Inspection
>   Service
> U.S. Department of Agriculture
> (City, State, Zip Code)

No government quarantine (and therefore no advance reservations or fees) and no foreign health certificate are required for birds taken out of the country if special arrangements are made in advance. Before leaving the United States you must get a health certificate for the bird from a veterinarian accredited by APHIS and make certain that the bird is identified with a tattoo or numbered leg band. The health certificate, with this identification number on it, must be presented at the time of reentry. While out of the country, you must keep your pet bird separate from other birds. Remember than only two psittacine or hook-billed birds per family per year may enter the United States. Birds returning to the United States may come in through any one of the nine ports of entry:

New York, New York 11430
Miami, Florida 33152
Laredo, Texas 78040
El Paso, Texas 79902
Nogales, Arizona 85621
San Ysidro, California 92073
Los Angeles, California (mailing
   address: Lawndale, CA 90261)
Honolulu, Hawaii 96850

There are also certain other specified ports of entry for psittacine or hook-billed birds, depending upon the time of arrival and other factors. Contact APHIS officials for information on this prior to leaving the country:

> Import-Export Staff
> Veterinary Services, APHIS
> U.S. Department of Agriculture
> Hyattsville, Maryland 20782

Pet birds may enter the United States from Canada on your signed statement that they have been in your possession for at least 90 days, were kept separate from other birds during that period, and are healthy. As with other countries, only two psittacine birds per family per year may enter the United States from Canada. Birds must be inspected by an APHIS veterinarian at designated ports of entry for land, air, and ocean shipments. These ports are subject to change, so for current information, contact APHIS officials at the address listed above.

Pet birds from Canada are not quarantined because Canada's animal disease control, eradication programs, and import rules are similar to those of the United States.

By the time you see parrots in a cage in a pet store, the worst is over, but they still miss their fellows, suffer from loneliness, and are filled with apprehension in a totally unfamiliar world. It should be obvious that such a bird needs all the consideration and forbearance we can muster during the adjusting period.

Domestically Raised African Gray Parrots

If you doubt whether you have the necessary patience to treat a bird with understanding during the long adjustment period often required by a parrot caught in the wild, you should look around for a domestically raised African Gray Parrot or get in touch with an experienced breeder of these birds. The easiest way of finding a breeder is to put an ad in an avicultural magazine or to inquire at an association of parrot breeders (for addresses, see page 61). Acquiring a parrot from a breeder often requires patience, too — but before you get your bird rather than after. African Gray Parrots do not reproduce on a predictable schedule, and not every mating cycle brings success. That is why you should write to a breeder and ask him or her to reserve you a youngster from one of the next broods. You may also have to travel some distance to pick up your bird because no responsible breeder will send birds by mail or by air. A domestically raised African Gray Parrot also costs more than an imported one. Raising parrots is more expensive than you might think. African Grays come into breeding condition only if they are kept under ideal conditions. They need high-quality food and sufficient living space with daylight, clean air, proper humidity and temperature, and room for exercise. Then there is the problem of finding a heterosexual pair of birds that take to each other. Many hopes

for parrot offspring have been dashed by mutual antipathy on the part of the potential parents. That is why an aviculturist needs to have a number of African Grays, so that pairs can form freely. Once there are eggs in the nest box, the breeder still cannot relax. The hen may fail to brood them reliably or may break some of the eggs. And then, when the young hatch, their successful development depends on whether they are fed regularly and enough. Even minor disturbances can cause the parent birds to abandon a nest, break eggs, stop feeding the nestlings, or even kill them.

That is why many aviculturists move the nestlings out of the nest box after a few days and hand-raise them. This means looking after the chicks for many weeks both day and night. Such a coddled African Gray Parrot chick grows up completely at ease with humans, and its future owner can count himself very lucky. But there is one factor to keep in mind: An African Gray that was raised by humans needs the company of humans as much as it needs food to eat and air to breathe. If it is neglected, is left alone too long, or does not receive enough affection, its reaction will be much more extreme than that of an African Gray Parrot directly from Africa.

The Band on a Parrot's Foot

Before an African Gray Parrot leaves the quarantine station, a band is put on one of its feet. The number and letters on the band are proof that the bird was quarantined and was examined by a USDA veterinarian. A

Buying and Housing a Parrot

breeder bands his nestlings as a guarantee that the birds were raised under official veterinary supervision. Every pet parrot is legally required to wear this band, but the owner should check the foot with the band frequently. If the flesh is beginning to grow around the band or if any abnormalities develop, the veterinarian should remove the band and attach a new one of appropriate size to the other foot.

Tips for Buying Birds

Buying a bird is always a somewhat risky matter because there are unscrupulous individuals in every line of business, including the pet trade. Your best bet for ending up with a healthy African Gray Parrot is to go to a reputable pet dealer or — if you are looking for a domestically raised bird — a respected breeder. No lover of animals should consider buying a bird by mail. If you buy an African Gray Parrot from a private source you should be extremely cautious unless you know the bird and its owner well. Ask in detail why the owner is selling his parrot. In many cases the owner wants to get rid of the bird because it has developed into a screamer or a feather plucker or is hopelessly timid as a result of improper treatment.

How to Tell a Healthy African Gray Parrot from a Sick One

A healthy African Gray Parrot is cheerful, looks around with interest, has smooth, uninterrupted plumage, eats and drinks, preens itself, and naps only intermittently.

You can tell a sick or maladjusted parrot by its apathy. It will usually sit in a corner of the cage with puffed up plumage and half-closed eyes. Droppings of abnormal consistency and shape (long, runny feces in the sand), dirty feathers around the cloaca, stuffed up nostrils, visible discharge from the nose, frequent sneezing, and continual scratching can all be signs of illness. Bare spots in the plumage — especially on the abdomen, breast, and back, which are covered with small feathers — may indicate feather plucking, in other words, a psychically unhealthy bird (see page 43).

The Age of the Bird

If you've decided that you'd like an African Gray Parrot, you should look for as young a bird as possible because it will almost certainly adjust more easily to a new environment than an older one will. You can find out a bird's exact age if you buy your parrot from a breeder because he knows the date when each of his birds hatched. Breeders sell young parrots as soon as they are able to feed themselves independently. Most imported African Gray Parrots are immature birds, too, but several months pass between the time of capture and the moment when a bird connects with its permanent owner (see page 13). The pet dealer generally knows, however, which import shipment a bird comes from and can make a fairly accurate guess of the bird's age.

How to Recognize a Young African Gray Parrot

Immature birds up to the age of about five to eight months have ash-gray irises, and the big, round "baby" eyes look black. Gradually the color of the iris lightens and turns whitish to pale yellow. Up to their first molt, juvenile African Gray Parrots have a somewhat shorter tail, and the under-tail coverts are sometimes partly gray.

You can also tell young African Gray Parrots by the fine pattern of the horny scales on the legs and by the smoothness of the upper mandible, the edges of which will hardly be chipped at all. After the juvenile molt is completed, young African Gray Parrots look exactly like their parents, and there is nothing that gives any indication of a bird's age.

Male or Female?

If you plan to keep a single bird, the question of whether you should choose a male or a female seems immaterial to me. There are no character differences between males and females; both have equal talents and learning abilities, and both become equally attached to people if they are treated properly. The question of sex is of importance only if you think that after the adjustment period you may want to find a mate for your bird with the intent of breeding your birds.

Sexing African Gray Parrots

Even for an expert it is not easy to tell the sex of an African Gray Parrot because the differences between the genders are minimal. A specialist who has examined many African Grays can tell with some accuracy what sex an African Gray Parrot is because the males have a slightly more powerful and larger bill than the females and a somewhat flatter, more "square" head. For serious breeding, aviculturists now have their African Gray Parrots

sexed by endoscopy or laparoscopy, an operation — performed with the bird under full anesthesia — in which a special optical instrument is introduced into the abdominal cavity through a small incision, and testes or ovaries can be observed.

Recently, some experts have stated that visually sexing African Grays is possible. According to Walter J. Rosskopf, Jr., females have a gray border of feathers around the vent; in males, these same feathers are solid red. Also, males have a solid dark-gray color extending from the chest to the tail, whereas the chest feathers of females fade to a lighter shade of gray toward the tail. Further, according to Matthew M. Vriends, the iris of the male is round; the female's, elliptical.

The Cage

Parrot cages are made in many sizes and styles, but only large pet stores carry more than a couple of models to choose from. Look around several pet stores and in the pet sections of large department stores and ask to see catalogs of cages and aviaries.

Size of the Cage

Many stores offer cages with a floor area of 18 x 18 inches (45 x 45 cm; see drawing on page 19). This is the absolute minimum size, and a cage of these dimensions is acceptable only if it is used exclusively as an occasional refuge, a sleeping place, and a feeding station. Keep in mind that an African Gray Parrot measures about 16 inches (40 cm), so that when it wants to turn around it has to sit in the exact center if its tail is not

Buying and Housing a Parrot

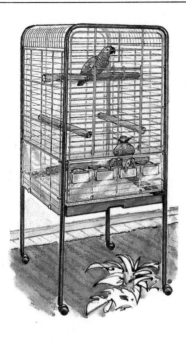

A parrot aviary measuring 30 x 30 x 65 inches (74 x 74 x 163 cm) is large enough to house two parrots as long as they are allowed exercise periods out of the cage.

going to rub against the grating. With a wing span of about 20 inches (50 cm), an African Gray Parrot can only spread one wing at a time in such a small cage. Cages much more appropriate for parrots have a floor area of 30 x 30 inches (74 x 74 cm; see drawing above), 32 x 20 inches (80 x 50 cm), or 44 x 28 inches (110 x 70 cm) and are usually sold as "parrot aviaries." If such a cage is 3 feet tall or more, it is quite adequate for one or two African Gray Parrots. Placed on a sturdy stand on wheels, it can be moved from one room to another or to a balcony or terrace.

What to Look for When Buying a Cage
● Never buy a round cage! African Gray Parrots kept in round cages show a high rate of psychic disturbances.
● The bars should run horizontally on at least two sides because African Grays like to climb and do so a lot. Horizontal bars offer a much better hold for their feet than vertical ones.
● The bars of the grating should be at least 1/8 inch (2.5–3 mm) thick and be spaced 1 to 1 1/4 inches (25–30 mm) apart. (African Grays can bend or break thinner bars, and too close spacing interferes with the view from the cage.)
● Try to find a cage with a flat top because parrots sometimes like to sit on top of their cage, and they tend to slide down the bars of a rounded top.
● The bottom pan should be made of a strong, unbreakable plastic. The bird should not be able to reach it when it is inside the cage because it may bite pieces off and perhaps swallow some of them with fatal consequences. (If necessary, insert a metal grate with narrow spacing between the grating part of the cage and the bottom pan.)
● The sand tray should be sturdy and slide in and out easily because it has to be cleaned daily. There is no need for a grate over the cage floor to keep the bird from touching its droppings. Such a grate is necessary only in case of certain diseases. Your parrot should be able to pick up sand, which it cannot do if there is a grate in the way.
● The cage door has to have a lock that is "beak-proof." A small padlock is best, and it can also serve to keep the cage door open. If a parrot spends most of its time on a climbing tree and the cage door closes acci-

Buying and Housing a Parrot

dentally, the bird is locked away from its food.

Basic Equipment for a Cage
A cage should have at least two unbreakable food dishes that are solidly mounted. Four would be better (for water, basic seed mixture, supplemental food, and sand or reserve food). Depending on the size of the cage, two or three perches are enough; they can consist of hardwood or, even better, of softer wood (which, however, has to be replaced fairly frequently) and have a diameter of about 1 1/4 inch (30 mm). The bird's toes should reach only about two thirds around the perch. Natural branches whose thickness varies between 3/4 and 2 inches (20–50 mm) are ideal. The perches have to be mounted securely and located where droppings cannot fall into the food dishes.

A parrot cage measuring 18 x 18 x 30 inches (45 x 45 x 75 cm) with a removable sand drawer. An African Gray Parrot living in a small cage like this needs to spend some of its time on a climbing tree or a free-standing perch.

An Indoor Aviary
An indoor aviary 80 inches wide, 40 inches deep, and 72 inches tall (200 x 100 x 180 cm) placed in a bright corner of the living room makes an ideal home for two parrots, unless you want to share the entire living room with your birds. In such an aviary there is room for a climbing tree, branches of different thicknesses, a bath tub, and perhaps even a nest box. But a single parrot kept in an indoor aviary is prevented from developing close contact with its caretaker and would, in spite of its luxurious quarters, grow lonely and bored and perhaps even suffer psychic illness. That is why you need two African Gray Parrots for an indoor aviary, assuming, of course, that the two like each other. The gender of the birds is irrelevant because two parrots either get along with each other or develop a mutual antipathy whether they are of the same or of the opposite sex. If you hope for offspring from your parrots, you should have your African Gray accurately sexed (see page 17) and make sure the second bird belongs to the opposite gender. But this by no means precludes the birds taking an instant dislike to each other and having to be separated again. Chances for offspring in an indoor aviary are slim because, as mentioned on page 15, there are many things that can interfere with successful reproduction. (On page 61 you will find some sources of information on the breeding of parrots.)

The Placement of the Cage

The cage should be located in a spot that is free of vibrations and that gets bright day-

Buying and Housing a Parrot

light. But it should not be right next to a window because in the winter windows radiate cold and in the summer the direct sun can cause heat stroke. A place right next to a radiator is not suitable either because the air is too hot and dry there. A parrot needs a permanent spot in a corner of the room so that it is not surrounded by activity on all sides. The cage should be placed at approximately adult chest level because parrots become nervous if anything goes on above their heads. If the cage is too high up, on the other hand, the contact between bird and humans is inhibited. The kitchen is generally not a good environment for a bird and should be considered only as a last resort. The temperature fluctuates too much there; cooking vapors and fat in the air are harmful to birds; and too many dangers lurk outside the cage (see List of Dangers, page 31). It is very important to find a draft-free spot; even the slightest draft can harm an African Gray. (Check out the chosen spot with a candle; any air movement will set the flame flickering.) Bright street lights shining into the room at night should also be avoided. (If there are no drapes or shutters, get some.) The parrot cage should also be at least 6 to 8 feet (2–2.5 m) away from the TV and be placed so that the bird is not directly in front of the screen.

Room temperature significantly affects the well-being of an African Gray Parrot. The bird will feel most comfortable at 64° to 68° F (18°–20° C). If the room is warmer than 64° F, the humidity should be at least 60%. If the temperature drops *slowly* below 64° F, this does not harm the parrot; it can be comfortable even at 59° F (15° C). But sudden and major temperature fluctuations are just as harmful as prolonged cold. Stale air, especially if saturated with cigarette smoke, or strong chemical odors are unhealthy for parrots.

The Climbing Tree

A climbing tree is a wonderful island of freedom for an African Gray, and you should get one if at all possible. Made up of natural branches, it provides excellent exercise for the bird's feet. It also offers lots of opportunity for climbing and keeping occupied, so that with any luck your parrot will refrain from attacking your furniture and upholstery with its strong beak. If set up properly, the climbing tree will also limit the area where droppings fall. To construct an ideal climbing tree, you should get a piece of a tree trunk about 1 foot in diameter and have it set into a

The primary occupation of an African Gray Parrot is gnawing. Only if your bird is supplied with enough fresh twigs and branches to keep its bill busy at all times can you hope that your furniture will remain unscathed.

very large tub (about 3 feet in diameter) by means of a metal ring or poured concrete. If there are tree limbs, cut them back so that they do not stick out beyond the tub. Then drill deep holes into the trunk at different intervals of 12 to 16 inches (30–40 cm). Stick oak, beech, or ash branches into the holes, using wedges, if necessary, to hold them in securely. The parrot will gnaw on the bark of the branches, which have to be replaced periodically. Chewing on the bark not only supplies valuable nutrients but also keeps the bird occupied. Pour a layer of bird sand into the tub. Droppings and other dirt can easily be removed from the sand with a slotted spoon.

A climbing tree you can construct yourself. A piece of tree trunk with some natural branches offers an African Gray Parrot opportunity for climbing and keeping busy. The trunk is placed in a large tub and set either in a block of cement or in gravel and sand.

Parrot Stands and Free-standing Perches

If you cannot set up a climbing tree, your parrot should have a free-standing perch outside the cage. Pet stores offer parrot stands that have several perches mounted at different heights. These stands are an acceptable substitute for a climbing tree, especially if the manufactured round perches are replaced with sturdy and securely mounted natural branches (see drawing, page 24). Some parrot stands have only one perch and come with a food dish and a chain and foot ring. *Important reminder*: A chained parrot can hurt itself seriously if it tries to fly or climb off the stand. Keeping a parrot on a chain is defensible only under unusual circumstances — and then only for short periods and with supervision. You may, for example, want to chain your parrot briefly if it is able to fly and you want to have it with you in the garden

or on a balcony. A parrot that is unable to fly should wear a foot ring and chain, too, as protection against falling if it is on a balcony or near an open window high above the ground. A better way to prevent accidents — one that offers more comfort to the bird and more peace of mind to the keeper — is to enclose the balcony or window with metal screening.

21

Keeping and Caring for an African Gray Parrot

Arrival at the New Home

When you pick up your African Gray Parrot at the pet store or from the breeder, everything at home should be ready. The cage should be in its permanent location, with a dish filled with water, the cage bottom covered with a layer of sand, and — just in case the bird should panic and thrash around wildly — a closely woven cloth handy to be thrown over the cage. Ask the person from whom you are buying your bird to give you enough of the seed mixture the parrot is used to to last for a few weeks, and ask what additional foods the bird has been given. This way the upsetting transition to a new environment is not aggravated by a simultaneous change in diet. Your parrot will be handed to you in a wooden transport box. Take it home instantly — in the winter in a warm car, and in the summer in the early morning or late afternoon to avoid the heat. When you get home, open the box and hold it against the open cage door. The bird will be eager to move from the dark box into the light. If it tries to climb up the outside wall instead of stepping into the cage, firmly place your flat hand over its head. The bird will shrink from the disagreeable contact with your hand and climb into the cage instead. Then close the door and lock it. Supply at least two dishes of the birdseed the parrot is used to. Then move some distance away from the cage and talk to the bird in a soothing voice. Leave it alone for a few hours. Remember that your naturally shy African Gray Parrot has to recover from the shock of being transported and needs a chance to look around without the added terror of strange people. Your bird may at this point be so frightened of humans that it doesn't dare eat in their presence. That is why you should leave it alone for a couple of hours at a time during the first few weeks.

Gradual Acclimation

At first your parrot will be terrified every time someone approaches the cage. It will flatten its feathers to look as slim as possible, scream loudly, flutter, spit or growl, cower in a corner, or cling desperately to the cage wall. In spite of this display of fear you have to change the food and water every day and remove the droppings. But all this can be done from the outside, and there is no need yet to busy yourself inside the cage.

Whenever you do anything near the cage, talk to the bird: Say its name several times and always use the same expressions. Get it used to a morning and evening greeting. And try to avoid things that are frightening to a bird, such as slamming doors or romping children and barking dogs. During this initial period the decibel level of daily family life should be toned down in the bird room.

The First Few Weeks with Your Bird

But even during this first period of special consideration for the bird, the keeper and his family should not tiptoe around the house anxiously trying not to make a sound. After all, the parrot will soon have to get used to the vacuum cleaner because in a few days the floor around the cage will be strewn with bits of birdseed and feathers. Use the vacuum first in the farthest corner from the cage and

Keeping and Caring for an African Gray Parrot

When an African Gray Parrot traverses an even surface, its large, somewhat pigeon-toed feet give its gait a droll and rather awkward look.

keep talking soothingly to the bird over the noise, coming closer very gradually. Even though the parrot may at first react with timidity or wild panic, the vacuum cleaner is something the bird will have to adjust to.

An inexperienced parrot owner is bound to feel a little squeamish the first time he has to reach into the cage to clean the droppings off the perches and grating. The easiest way to accomplish this is to have some paper towels handy and clean up while the droppings are still fresh. Soft droppings come off easily, but once they harden they have to be scraped off, which will alarm your African Gray even more. Stay calm even if the bird hacks at you! If you jump back, this will signal to the bird that its attack was successful. The hacking won't really hurt and is more of a test of courage for the bird. To really hurt you it would have to get very close

to your hand and bite hard, which it won't dare do — yet. But try to watch out so that the beak hits only the back of your hand and not a finger. After this first experiment you should reach into the cage at least once a day. This way the parrot learns that your hand is nothing to be afraid of. Offer a piece of fruit each time or some treat the bird knows and likes. If it doesn't take it, leave it in a food dish. The day the parrot takes the treat cautiously from your hand, you will know that you have come a long way.

A Good Night's Rest

African Gray Parrots come from near the equator in Africa. The nearly constant length of the days and nights there allows the birds to search for food nearly twelve hours a day. They need this long forage period to thrive, and in captivity they should not spend too much time in the dark during the winter. Turn on a nonglaring light near the cage to lengthen the short winter days. If you are not able to switch on the light reliably, you can install a timer or a combination dimmer/timer (available at stores that sell electric appliances). I also recommend using a night light (with a 10 or 15 watt bulb), but do not place it too close to the cage. If a bird is frightened in the middle of the night by an unusual noise like a car door slamming, brakes squealing, or a thunderstorm, it may try to fly off and can hurt itself by fluttering wildly in the small cage. The night light helps the bird see where it is, and it is not so likely to feel threatened by an unusual noise if its surroundings look normal. If the parrot still flutters nervously at night for some reason, you should get up and talk to it soothingly in dim light.

Keeping and Caring for an African Gray Parrot

Should one put a cloth over the cage at night or not? I personally think not. If a bright street light shines into the room, drapes or blinds will shut it out more effectively. If you have to work in the room with bright lights late into the night, the cage can be in relative darkness as long as you aim the lamp directly at your work table. But you will certainly want to cover the cage with a closely woven cloth to keep out drafts or the winter cold when you air the room.

Check to see if the parrot is in its habitual sleeping place before you turn off the main light and leave the room for the night. If the bird has to retire to its sleeping place in the dark, there will be much fumbling and thrashing about.

Freedom of Movement Outside the Cage

When your parrot begins to show interest in its surroundings and when its initial fearfulness has subsided, you can begin to let it spend some time — an hour or two — outside the cage. Make sure that all doors and windows are shut and that no one will burst into the room unexpectedly. (The bird might be sitting near the door and could be hurt or badly frightened by the door being flung open.) Windows without curtains can also spell disaster because an African Gray that can fly will make straight for the light. A crash against the window glass can result in serious injuries or even death from a broken neck. If you cannot hang curtains, you will have to teach your bird that the glass is an invisible barrier. During your bird's first free-flying sessions, lower the shades or

A free-standing parrot perch (available at pet stores) with round dowels. The dowels can be replaced with natural branches as shown here. Mount the branches as shown in the inset drawings.

Venetian blinds to leave about 12 inches (30 cm) of the window uncovered. Then raise the blinds a couple of inches every day. Stay in the room for the first few times while the parrot is out of its cage so that you can help if needed.

You cannot predict a parrot's first response to an open cage door. Most African Gray Parrots approach it with curiosity and, eager for more exercise, immediately use the opportunity to climb on top of the cage. But perhaps your bird will be so taken aback by the unexpected change that it sits glued to its perch for a while, trying to gather courage for a first venture outside. Sooner or later, however, every bird will take off. This is the moment when you find out whether your parrot can fly or whether its flight feathers were clipped after capture.

An African Gray Parrot that cannot fly will flutter pitifully or perhaps tumble to the floor the first time it tries its wings. At this point it will need your help. Have a small ladder (available at pet stores) ready so that the bird can climb back into its cage. With a bird that cannot fly, it is also a good idea to place a sturdy, permanent ladder at the foot of the climbing tree so that it can always manage without your help.

A parrot with wings that are intact will take to the air and, if it is lucky, avoid collisions in the limited space available to it. If all goes well, it will land on some high perch, such as a shelf, a lamp, a curtain rod, or whatever else may be handy. But if you have already set up a climbing tree, your parrot will probably make straight for it. And if there is a way to get from the climbing tree back to the cage "on foot," the return trip will be unproblematic. If, however, your parrot begins to feel uneasy on some perch high up in the room and is reluctant to venture back, you should simply wait patiently. Sooner or later hunger will win out over fear. If worse comes to worst, a night spent outside the cage is less harmful for the parrot than being shooed off its high seat by whatever means. Never reach with your hands for an African Gray that is not yet tame. This gesture will shake the bird's budding trust in humans and have lasting consequences. *Another important reminder*: The only way to try to prevent your parrot from leaving beak marks along the edges of wooden furni-

African Gray Parrots are regular acrobats. Here a trusting bird is hanging upside down from its keeper's hand.

ture and on upholstery, carpets, wallpaper, drapes, and clothes is to keep the bird busy on a climbing tree, lavish affection on it, and not leave it alone much. You cannot "train" an African Gray. It is possible to teach it a few things, but the forbidding "No! No!" has to be sounded immediately every time temptation arises, which means that you have to be present constantly. The best and only successful method of "education" is to treat the bird with consistent patience and understanding. Rewards are appreciated, and the bird will try to earn them with appropriate behavior. Punishment, on the other hand, is incomprehensible and frightening to an African Gray Parrot. In my opinion, African Grays are unable to comprehend the connection between something they did and an unpleasant experience that follows.

Keeping and Caring for an African Gray Parrot

Toys and Entertainment

Even if your African Gray Parrot spends most of its days on a climbing tree, you still have to work patiently to help it overcome its innate fear of humans. Since the bird has been receiving treats from your hand every day, it has probably concluded that you are not too dangerous. The next step in taming the reluctant pet is to initiate gentle body contact. Try stroking your African Gray's head lightly with a little stick and maybe even brushing the nape feathers up slightly. Eventually the bird will allow you to use your finger for this, but you will still have to wait a while before it invites you to scratch its head by lowering it.

Your parrot also needs a few objects to keep it busy. African Gray Parrots vary a lot in what they consider entertaining and what they ignore. If you can, you should supply your bird with fresh twigs — rinsed under hot water and dried — every day to gnaw on. Maple, beech, oak, alder, ash, elderberry, unsprayed fruit trees, poplar, willow, and hawthorn are all fine. For entertainment you can offer various items: a thick piece of rope with a knot tied in it; a short, rustproof chain made of big links; wooden curtain rings; leather dice shakers; old postcards; the cardboard tubes inside rolls of toilet paper, or wooden toys that are sold at pet stores. Simply put whatever toy you are offering within the parrot's reach or tie it to the climbing tree. The bird itself will decide whether and when to investigate it.

Reminder: Don't give your bird anything made of plastic, other synthetic materials, cellulose, or glass. Empty containers that had harmful or poisonous substances in them may prove fatal if gnawed on.

The Talking Parrot

A truly tame parrot will be eager for close physical contact with people. It will let itself be petted, scratched, and held; it will climb up on its human partner's shoulder and even groom and feed that partner. But long before this stage is reached, the bird will establish initial contact with its human companions by means of its voice. Its shrill calls and screeching gradually become less frequent. But even African Gray Parrots that have lived in aviaries or in human families for years still whistle a little tune that seems to be part of their innate repertoire. This "tune" sounds something like "hee-o-heet" with the second note lower in pitch than the other two. This whistling is not very loud and is so easily imitated by humans that we fall into it almost automatically and use it to establish our first vocal communication with our birds. Depending on their moods, African Grays also produce other sounds like beak cracking, clicking sounds, spitting, growling, a kind of drawn out chirping, and imitations of sounds they often hear, such as someone's cough. Gradually bits of human speech and entire words are incorporated into the parrot's vocalizations as well.

Tips for the "Speech Lessons"

When you hear your parrot utter wordlike sounds, you should support its efforts. Call out a clearly enunciated short greeting, such

African Gray Parrots are expert climbers. This bird is making its way across the curtains with acrobatic dexterity.

Keeping and Caring for an African Gray Parrot

as "Hello, Nicky!" or "Come here, Sweetie!" whenever you enter the bird's room. Offer treats with the same words every time, perhaps "Here's something good!" When the parrot lowers its head to be scratched, say "Come pet me." Always praise your parrot with the same words — for instance, "That's a good boy!" And of course you greet the bird every day with a "Good morning" and leave it in the evening with a "Good night." The more interest your parrot shows in these "conversations," the more often you should repeat the expressions it has already learned. Gradually introduce more and more word combinations. Of course the parrot has to be in a mood to listen. If it is executing a daring climbing maneuver or examining some object, it will pay little attention to you. But you'll soon figure out at what times your parrot is a willing student. One important rule is to immediately repeat word fragments or improperly uttered words correctly and slowly. In the evening, when the parrot has already retired to its sleeping place, repeat the entire learned vocabulary once more and especially the words that are in the process of being mastered.

An African Gray's talent for mimicry is particularly delightful when — thanks to its excellent memory — it is able to produce sounds, words, and phrases in their proper context. All it may take is for someone to pull a handkerchief out of a pocket before the sounds of loud nose-blowing come from the parrot. Or the bird will respond to the ring of

African Gray Parrots loose in the apartment.
Above: African Gray Parrots flying about; even a slippery metal railing presents no obstacle.
Below: An unusual friendship among animals: a cat and some young African Gray Parrots sharing a meal.

Almost any African Gray Parrot likes to have its head scratched. Use just one finger, not the entire hand.

the telephone with a cheerful "Hello!" Konrad Lorenz recalls how Professor Otto Koehler's African Gray Parrot used to say in a benevolent, beery voice, "Well, good-bye now" every time a visitor rose to leave.

The Tame Parrot

Vocal exchange with its caretaker or other members of the household always gives an African Gray a sense of safety and strengthens its trust. Perhaps you are at the stage where your bird lets you scratch its head now and then and has learned to associate the human hand with good things. But making it completely hand or shoulder tame will still take a lot of patience. Setbacks are inevitable. In the middle of having its head scratched tenderly, an excessively sensitive parrot may suddenly hack at you for no discernable reason. You may have no idea what startled or upset the bird. In a case like this, always remember that an African Gray never acts out of meanness, malice, cunning, resentment, or other motives we know from human intercourse; the bird's behavior is probably triggered by memories of earlier improper or bad treatment.

Keeping and Caring for an African Gray Parrot

Advice for Hand-Taming

There is no one surefire way to tame an African Gray Parrot. The advice that follows is what I have gleaned from parrot owners and books.

● Start offering a favorite treat on the back of your hand instead of holding it directly in front of the bird's beak; then let the bird get it from your arm, your shoulder, and eventually out of your lap.

● Get the parrot used to climbing onto a little stick you hold up to it; this way you can, if necessary, carry your parrot to its cage or climbing tree without having to grasp it with your hands.

● Always let the bird approach you rather than vice versa. When it comes up to you, don't pet it immediately but talk to it first and perhaps reward it with something good to eat.

The well-known parrot expert Rosemary Low writes that only few parrots become truly tame and that the main reason for this is improper treatment and too little affection. Karl-Herbert Delpy advises not to give up on an African Gray that has been acclimated for less than a year. From my own experience, I would say that some African Grays take more than one year to become tame. And no two African Grays are exactly alike. Many will happily get onto their caretaker's arm or shoulder, use people to climb on, or let themselves be carried around on a stick. Others hate being touched but are tame in their own fashion, and are completely devoted to their keeper. My African Gray, Moses, for instance, refuses to this day to get on my shoulder, although I have spent hours crouching in front of him to make the move less threatening. He generally avoids all physical contact — except head scratching — but clearly enjoys it if he is grasped gently from behind, pressed against my chest, and then petted at length. By playing with your bird a lot, scratching its head, giving it all kinds of things to play with, and being constantly around it, you can help your African Gray Parrot to get used to people and their world — though this may take a very long time. Its timid reserve will gradually melt away, and in the end your parrot will feel completely integrated into its new "flock." This is all you should expect, for birds are not "pets"; they cannot be treated like dolls — they are freedom-loving creatures that resent being pressured but are happy to bestow their affection on people when they feel like it.

Protection Against Dangers

The List of Dangers on page 31 enumerates dangers and possible accidents and offers suggestions on how to avoid them.

Making Windows and Doors Safe

The greatest danger for all birds in captivity is flying away. How to keep your African Gray from escaping depends largely on your habits and on your particular situation. If you love fresh air from open windows and like to keep the door to the balcony or terrace open in the summer, or if you cannot rely on all the members of your household to be conscientious about closing doors and windows, you should install strong metal screens at windows and doors leading to the outside. Caution: Venetian blinds in front of open or even cracked windows are no safeguard

Keeping and Caring for an African Gray Parrot

List of Dangers

Source of Danger	Effects	How to Avoid
Bathroom	Escape through open window; drowning in toilet, filled sink, or bathtub. Poisoning from cleansers or other chemicals.	Keep parrot out; never leave bathroom door open.
Electric wires	Electric shock from chewing or biting through wires.	Run wires behind walls, under carpets, or behind furniture, or protect with metal covers. Unplug.
Poisons	Poisoning from lead, verdigris, rust, nicotine, pans coated with plastic, cleansers, plant pesticides, mercury. Also harmful: pencil lead, inserts for ballpoint pens and magic markers, alcohol, coffee, hot spices.	Remove all poisonous objects and substances and store out of parrot's reach. Don't forget lead weights in drapes.
Windows and glass doors	Bird flies against glass, sustains concussion or broken neck.	Hang curtains or teach parrot awareness of the invisible border (see page 24).
Glue	Death from inhaling evaporating solvents.	When using glue (in repairs, crafts, laying floor coverings), remove all animals from the room and air thoroughly before bringing them back.
Kitchen	Steam and cooking odors affect air passages; overheated kitchen and necessary airing lead to colds and other illnesses. Burns from burners that are turned off but still hot and from food in uncovered dishes.	Don't keep bird in kitchen; or, if you do, air frequently and briefly — watch out for drafts. Put pots of water on unused hot burners; cover pots.
Plants	Poisoning, often deadly; for plants, shrubs, and trees that are poisonous, see page 35.	Don't keep poisonous house plants; don't give bird branches from poisonous trees or shrubs to gnaw on.
Doors	Bird gets caught and crushed if door is opened or shut carelessly. May also escape.	Only constant watchfulness can prevent accidents and escape.
Cigarettes	Smoke-laden air is harmful, and nicotine is poisonous.	It is best if no one smokes near the bird. At least air regularly (avoid drafts). Keep cigarettes out of bird's reach.
Drafts	Colds, pneumonia.	Avoid drafts at all cost! Check that there are no drafts near cage (see page 20); cover cage or move it to another room when airing.

against escape. African Gray Parrots have no trouble climbing up on blinds or drapes and pushing their way through an opening. They are also adept at opening doors and casement windows that are not closed tight.

Clipping the Wings

If you are unwilling or unable to install screens, you will have to curtail your parrot's flying ability to prevent its escape. But don't experiment with this. Have a veterinarian, a breeder, or a competent pet dealer trim the wings for the first time and watch closely how it's done. Opinion about how the flight feathers are to be cut varies so widely that I feel I should explain some of the different ways.

Clipping Methods To Be Avoided: Some experts tell you to clip only one wing. The disadvantage of this is that the bird can flap the untampered wing but is unable to maintain its balance. Fluttering to the ground in this lopsided fashion has led to some fatal accidents. Another possibility is to cut back the flight feathers on both sides. The disadvantage here is that the bird looks disfigured even if the first two primaries are left whole.

Recommended Method of Clipping: In this method, which is the one you should insist on, the flight feathers are cut on both sides with sharp scissors — never pulled, which would be pure and unnecessary cruelty. Cut off every other primary and secondary just over 1 inch (3 cm) from the skin: Leave the outermost primary as is, cut the next feather, leave the third, and so on. This does not deprive the parrot entirely of its wing power but disables it enough to prevent escape. In an emergency the bird is still able

to flutter away from danger, and severe falls are avoided. The clipping will have to be repeated once or twice a year because during molt the feather stumps are shed along with the rest of the plumage, and the new feathers all grow back to full length. So keep a watchful eye out to notice when the bird regains its full flying power.

Essential Hygiene

An African Gray Parrot keeps clean by spending several hours every day grooming or preening its entire plumage. Patiently it pulls one feather after another through its bill, removing any dust on it and smoothing it. Several times in the course of the preening the bird shakes itself vigorously to get rid of even the tiniest motes of down or dust and any feathers that may have become loose.

The Shower Bath

Parrots living in captivity miss the fine, warm spray of daily tropical rains that penetrates through the branches and foliage of the trees where the birds live. You should make up for this by showering lukewarm water on your parrot — if it is tame or at least no longer afraid of you — from a plant mister twice a week. (Be sure the plant mister never had insecticides in it!) The parrot may at first be frightened, but after a few times it will undoubtedly begin to appreciate and welcome the shower bath. A bird should never be soaked to the skin; the moisture should reach only the outer feathers. If an African Gray really enjoys the bath, it may twist and bend, raise its wings, and perhaps

Keeping and Caring for an African Gray Parrot

A parrot spends several hours a day preening itself, turning and twisting to reach everywhere, including the tail feathers that need smoothing out.

even hang from a branch head down to expose all parts of its body to the water.

If your parrot lives in a climbing tree, showering presents no problems. A parrot in a cage can be sprayed by setting the cage on a towel with the bottom pan removed. Or perhaps your African Gray will take a regular bath in a bathtub. For this you can use a heavy pottery bowl with about 2 inches (5 cm) of lukewarm water in it.

Routine Cleaning Chores

The requirements of hygiene impose a few cleaning chores on you. Food dishes should be emptied every day, rinsed under hot water without soap or cleanser, dried, and filled again. Use a slotted spoon to remove droppings and leftover bits of food from the sand at the bottom of the cage. Then replenish sand as necessary. Perches and branches that are filthy have to be scraped with a knife and then rubbed clean with a damp cloth.

The floor around the cage also has to be cleaned every day.

Once a week, both the sand drawer and the bottom pan of the cage should be washed in hot water and dried. Add nothing to the water except a disinfectant such as F. Lysol, manufactured by Lehn and Fials Products division of Sterling Drug (dilution: 4 ounces per gallon of water); or One-Stroke Environ (the official disinfectant of the USDA) manufactured by Vestal (dilution: 1/2 ounce per gallon of water). Every three or four weeks the entire cage, the climbing tree, the cage stand, and everything else the parrot uses should be disinfected. The metal grating of the cage (the cage minus the plastic pan at the bottom) should first be rinsed off with hot water in the bathtub. Cages or aviaries too large to move can be washed off with hot water and one of the above disinfectants.

Diet

The Basic Birdseed Mixture

Pet stores as well as seed stores sell packaged mixed birdseed that satisfies the nutritional needs of African Gray Parrots. The mixture is usually made up of 15% striped black-and-white sunflower seeds; 10% each of buckwheat, canary grass seed (or white seed), and whole rice; 5% each of hulled oats, barley, wheat, peanuts, corn flakes, mynah pellets, white millet, and kibbled corn; and 3% crushed red peppers. The 2% whole corn that is sometimes included is generally ignored or only nibbled on by parrots. Corn should be soaked for a few hours before it is given to parrots. Using the proportions given above, keepers of several parrots can make up their own birdseed mixture.

It is extremely important that all the ingredients be of excellent quality. They should be stored properly and not too long, and they must never be spoiled, rancid, or dirty. When buying packaged seed, check the date stamped on the package. Never buy seed that was packed more than six months earlier because normally several weeks or even months elapse between the harvest and the final processing. Spot test some sunflower seeds from every package you buy by removing the shells. The same goes for nuts in the shell, if there are any. Chew a kernel to see if it tastes rancid. Mildew is easy to detect, and anything that is rotting smells. Insect pests (weevils and flour beetles) are present if clumps of kernels are stuck together or if fine, webby threads are found in the mixture. If there is anything wrong with the birdseed, throw out the entire package or else take it back to the store where you purchased it. In any case, don't feed it to your parrot. Even when everything looks all right, you should sprout a few seeds from each package to check on nutritional value. If about 60% of the seeds sprout, the birdseed is nutritionally adequate, but if only about 20% sprout, the mixture will not supply enough of the essential vitamins, and you should try a different product.

Sprouting Seeds

When viable seeds absorb water, a chemical reaction takes place that causes the seeds to sprout. As the seeds swell, vitamins, minerals, and trace elements are released, causing an increase in nutritional value, which becomes even greater as the sprouts develop. Sunflower seeds, hulled oats, and wheat are easiest to sprout and are especially nutritious when sprouted. Cover about 1 tablespoon of the kernels with lukewarm water and let stand for 24 hours. Then rinse under lukewarm water, put in a shallow saucer and cover with a plate (don't cover with plastic because if there is no air exchange the kernels begin to get moldy). After 24 hours the swollen kernels can be fed to the parrot, but if you wait another 24 hours, their nutritional value will be much higher. Before giving sprouts or soaked kernels to your parrot, rinse them once more well under cold water and drain excess water by putting them on a paper towel.

Important reminder: Soaked and sprouted kernels spoil quickly. Give some in the morning in a separate dish and remove what is not eaten after one or two hours. This way the bird will not eat food that is beginning to rot and might cause illness.

How long should you go on giving your parrot sprouts? Let the bird decide. Once it has gotten used to sprouted seeds, it will be eager to get this treat for a few days; but after a while the bird's appetite will diminish. When the sprouts are hardly touched anymore, it is time to give the parrot a rest from sprouts for a few weeks.

But every so often you should reintroduce sprouted seeds into your African Gray's diet. They are a valuable strengthening food that is especially important when birds molt, when they sit on eggs, and when they raise offspring. Sprouts are also an ideal addition to the menu during the winter and in early spring when fresh fruits and vegetables are scarcer.

Fruit, Vegetables, and Greens

A birdseed mixture is only a substitute food for an African Gray Parrot and does not by itself constitute an adequate diet. In the wild, African Grays live primarily on fruits that are not available in our stores. That is why it is so important that we offer our captive parrots fresh fruit, vegetables, and greens several times a day, even though, being unfamiliar, these foods will at first be ignored or dropped quickly after a short investigation by the tongue. Remember that African Gray Parrots are archconservative and suspicious of anything new. They learn only slowly that the things we offer them are worth a try. But keep hanging some greens near the perch and offering bits of salad makings and raw vegetables that you have on hand for your own meals. The more variety the parrot has to choose from, the more likely it will find something to its taste. But remember: Nothing should come directly from the refrigera-

tor, let alone be half frozen. Wash fruit, vegetables, and greens carefully in lukewarm water to get rid of pesticides or traces of car exhaust that might be present. Fruit and vegetables should be peeled because the chemicals are usually on or just beneath the skin. Nothing intended for a bird should be moldy or decayed. If the fresh food is left untouched for several hours, replace it with something different.

Suitable raw vegetables: Eggplant, endive, cucumbers, kohlrabi, fresh sweet corn (about 1 1/2 inches of an ear per day; freeze the remainder of the ear), swiss chard, carrots, green peppers (remove the white ribs and the seeds), asparagus, spinach, tomatoes, zucchini, and hydroponic oats.

Unsuitable vegetables: Green beans, any kind of cabbage, Brussels sprouts, supermarket lettuce.

Suitable fruit: Apples, pineapple, apricots, bananas, all kinds of berries, cherries, kiwi fruit, pumpkins along with seeds, tangerines, mangoes, melons along with seeds, oranges, papayas, peaches, plums, grapes.

Suitable wild fruit and herbs: Rowan berries, rosehips, ripe elderberries, firethorn and hawthorn berries, shepherd's purse (leaves and blossoms), wild millet (handfuls with half ripe seeds), cress, parsley, chickweed (by the handful), velvet grass (by the handful and with half ripe seeds).

Important reminder: Don't gather wild plants along the roadside or near cultivated fields that have been sprayed with pesticides.

Unsuitable or poisonous plants: All *Aconitum* and *Ameryllis* species, *Colchicum* species, henbane, nux vomica, baneberry, honey locust, all *Dieffenbachia* and *Helleborus* species, fool's parsley, hyacinth, corn cockle, periwinkle, privet, all plants belonging to the nightshade family (Solanaceae), narcissus, oleander, spindle tree, saxifrage, primroses, jimsonweed, philodendron, rhododendron, spurge, Japanese yew, lantana, etc.

Valuable supplemental foods: Beechnuts; peanuts in the shell; hazelnuts in cracked shells; pine nuts; walnuts in cracked shells; cedar nuts in cracked shells; hard-boiled egg yolk (no more often than twice a week); finely chopped dried prawn; dog biscuits; cookies without chocolate or frosting; buds of unsprayed fruit trees, alders, elderberry, or willows; low-fat cottage cheese mixed with hard-boiled egg yolk; unflavored bread crumbs; grated carrot; chopped herbs; calcium (no more often than twice a week, but can be given daily as rearing food); raisins that are washed and dabbed dry; zwieback.

Branches for gnawing: Make sure these have not been sprayed and were not picked near highways. Maple, beech, alder, ash, elderberry, basswood, poplar, mountain ash, willow, hawthorn.

Unsuitable or poisonous branches: Acacia, birch, yew, laburnum, viburnum, holly, and all conifers.

Drinking Water; Vitamin and Mineral Supplements

An African Gray Parrot should always have fresh, clean drinking water available. On hot summer days the water should be changed twice a day. Use tap water or non-carbonated mineral water.

The sand on the cage floor is there not just for hygienic reasons but also as an aid to

Food dishes with convenient clamps to attach to the cage wall.

digestion. The parrot picks up grains of sand (grit) that help grind down the food in the gizzard. Sand also supplies minerals. If a grate prevents the parrot from reaching the cage floor, sand should be offered in a dish. Hard stones for sharpening bills, cuttle bone, or natural lime stones help the parrot keep its bill in shape and supply the necessary calcium. But since many African Gray Parrots either ignore cuttle bone and stones or make a game of biting them to bits, a calcium supplement should be sprinkled over the birdseed, on pieces of fruit, or on the cottage-cheese mixture. Pet stores sell calcium supplements designed especially for large parrots.

During the winter months, as well as during molt, in situations of stress, and when birds are breeding, it is a good idea to add a multivitamin (bought at a drugstore or a pet store) to the drinking water or the soft food. This ensures that the birds are well supplied with these important nutrients.

Amounts of Food

The more fruit and vegetables a bird consumes, the less birdseed it will eat. But seeds

African Gray Parrots are virtuoso acrobats. With the aid of its bill this parrot will manage to climb back up on the hand.

Diet

should always be available and in good supply. A parrot should never get so hungry that it then stuffs itself greedily. It is possible for a parrot to go hungry even when there is plenty of food in the dish simply because a layer of empty hulls hides the seeds underneath. That is why you should check twice a day, remove the debris on top, and add fresh birdseed.

How much food should you give? Put a heaping tablespoon of birdseed into each of two dishes to start with. Later, remove the empty hulls and add about two teaspoons at a time. Hang a small bunch of greens in the cage twice a day and give about a cupful of fruit and other vegetables. Raisins, nuts, zwieback, and other foods rich in calories should be given sparingly and mostly as treats to strengthen contact with the parrot or as an aid in taming it.

An African Gray Parrot that has enough exercise and keeps busy does not eat out of boredom and does not get fat. If you observe your African Gray's eating habits as well as its behavior and droppings, you will be able to tell whether or not the food offered agrees with the bird. Fresh sweet corn can initially cause diarrhea, but once the parrot gets used to this nutritious food, the droppings return to normal.

Reminder: It is crucial that the parrot find food when it first wakes up in the morning so that it can replenish its energies after the night's rest. Clean the dishes and refill them for breakfast the night before.

My African Gray Parrot, Moses, and my dog, Ailyn, have made friends.

Food from the Table

Many tame parrots regard the family dinner as the high point of the day and look forward to it. If given a chance, they climb onto the table or on the back of a chair near the table to get a tidbit now and then. If you enjoy these visits, have some food ready that is good for the bird. But only a few of the things we eat should be given to African Grays: pasta, potatoes, and vegetables (except cabbage) that were cooked with very little salt and are cool; veal and chicken bones with almost no meat but some gristle; lightly toasted bread; bread crusts; hard-boiled egg; dry cake.

Forbidden are: salted or spicy foods, and pure fat or hidden fat as in sausage, meat, cheese, and milk. No alcoholic beverages, coffee, or black tea should ever be given to a bird.

A tame African Gray Parrot will want a taste of anything its keeper eats or drinks. You may let your bird have a sip of water or fruit juice (no carbonated drinks) from your glass, but never give it anything with alcohol in it.

Diseases and How to Keep Your Parrot Healthy

African Gray Parrots are often said to be quite robust and to stay healthy for a long time even under adverse conditions. But I (and the veterinarians I know) feel that this is not an accurate view. African Gray Parrots normally have a long life expectancy, and disturbances in the basic life functions do not become evident as quickly as they do in smaller birds with shorter life spans. Because African Grays survive abuse better, it may take longer before the caretaker realizes that something is wrong. Most of the health problems an African Gray Parrot is subject to are the result of faulty conditions or diet, and the harm they do is just as serious and long lasting as that of the much feared infectious diseases. For African Grays, as for any other pet, proper conditions and care and a correct diet are the crucial factors in preventing sickness. If a bird should get sick in spite of excellent care, its basically resilient nature justifies hope that prompt treatment and conscientious nursing will lead to recovery.

The Molt

The molt is a necessary process in which old, worn out feathers are replaced. It is by no means a sickness, but it does represent a strain on the parrot's physical system, and special care is required during this time to forestall possible problems.

During the molt the bird spends more time than usual pecking at its feathers and preening itself. It pulls out feathers that are loose and that itch. The new feathers are at first enveloped in a thin sheath. Once these little "feather spears" are 1 to 1 1/2 inches long, the bird tries to speed up the process of ridding itself of these sheaths by pecking at the plumage.

If several of the large flight feathers come out at the same time, the flying capacity of an African Gray may be temporarily curtailed — assuming the bird was able to fly before the onset of the molt. During this period when the parrot cannot quite trust its wings, accidents are common. When the flight feathers are growing back in, the keeper has to remember in good time that a parrot that previously had clipped wings will now be able to fly (see Clipping the Wings, page 32). In any case caution is in order.

Reminder: You should assume that something is wrong and consult a veterinarian if there is excessive feather loss during molt to the extent that bald spots appear or if the new feathers are misshapen or grow in so slowly that the bird almost looks as though it had been plucked. These may be signs of deficiency diseases, parasite infestation, or serious mistakes in environmental conditions or diet.

A Sick African Gray Parrot

If your African Gray gets sick, you will soon know it from the changes in its behavior. A sick parrot is apathetic, often sits resting on both legs, tucks its head into the lightly puffed up back feathers, and keeps its eyes partially or completely shut. When not asleep, it stares into space with dull eyes, yawns frequently, ignores treats, and generally lacks appetite. Sometimes a bird is thirstier than usual. Generally, illness is also accompanied by changes in the droppings,

Diseases and How to Keep Your Parrot Healthy

which may be mushy to watery, foamy, fermenting, or discolored. If you also notice weakness, as when a bird is half lying on its perch instead of sitting up straight; if there is a discharge from the nostrils or a slimy secretion from the bill; if the eyes tear; if the bird breathes noisily or shallowly; if there are changes in the beak or on the legs; or if there are bald spots, these are all unmistakable signs of illness. Keep the parrot quiet and warm at an even temperature and take it to the veterinarian as quickly as you can.

First Measures to Take

If you see one day that your African Gray looks sick, has been hurt, or is disabled in any way, you will have to initiate the first measures of treatment or apply first aid.

Infrared Radiation

I would recommend to anyone who keeps birds to get a heat lamp with an infrared bulb (250 watts). The warmth such a lamp radiates has a beneficial effect in treating many minor and even major illnesses. (But watch out: If there is any sign of cramps or paralysis, discontinue use of the lamp and take the bird to the veterinarian immediately.) Set the lamp up outside the cage and close the cage door. If the parrot should touch the lamp, severe burns could result. The lamp should be about 12 to 20 inches (30–50 cm) away from the cage and aimed in such a way that the bird can get away from its rays if it gets too hot. The temperature should never rise above 104° F (40° C). If the bird seems to be more comfortable with the heat lamp, you can leave it on for several hours or even

Shining an infrared heat lamp on a sick bird can have a beneficial effect in treating many diseases. The lamp should be aimed at only half the cage so that the bird can get away from the warm rays.

overnight. But if you use it for long periods, adequate humidity has to be supplied. Place a bowl with hot water between the cage and the lamp and, as it cools, replace it with fresh hot water every hour or so. If the bird does not obviously improve, it is better to turn the lamp off after about half an hour and expose the bird to it again for a brief period three or four times a day. When you turn off the lamp, the temperature should not drop suddenly. You can achieve a gradual cooling down by turning on a regular light bulb.

The use of a heat lamp should never be the only treatment of a sick parrot. Warmth alone will not cure anything but very minor ailments. Always take your parrot to the veterinarian to be on the safe side.

Superficial Injuries and Bleeding

Parrots sometimes get small lacerations on the feet or, more rarely, on the body. If one of these minor wounds bleeds, press some

41

styptic cotton against it and wash it with lukewarm water or strained camomile tea as soon as the bleeding has stopped. If a wound continues to bleed profusely, a major blood vessel is probably damaged. In this case you should tie the styptic cotton against the wound with a bandage and take the bird to the veterinarian as soon as you can.

Parrots with clipped wings sometimes land so awkwardly when they flutter to the ground that the shaft of a clipped feather may hit against an object or against the floor so hard that the feather breaks and the base of it, which is supplied with blood, is injured. Thick drops of blood ooze from the shaft. Usually the bleeding stops after a minute or so. If the damaged feather is not shed after a day or two, you should have a veterinarian remove it.

Fractures

Any fractures should be treated by a veterinarian. Only he knows how to bandage a broken wing or leg properly, and he also should remove the bandage. Until you can take the bird, don't leave it alone, and keep it very quiet (in a darkened room or by throwing a dark cloth over the cage). After the trip to the veterinarian, mount a perch about 2 inches (5 cm) above the cage bottom, which is covered with a thick layer of sand (remove the bottom grate if there is one). The bird should be able to reach the birdseed and the drinking water easily from this perch.

Overgrown Claws and Excessive Growth of the Beak

If the claws of your parrot get obviously

longer than they should be and they get caught in things repeatedly (this can lead to serious injuries), they have to be trimmed. It is best to let a veterinarian or a pet dealer specializing in birds do this because African Gray Parrots have dark claws in which the blood vessels do not show up well. If you cut too close to a blood vessel, you may pinch a nerve, which is painful; and if you cut into a vein or artery, heavy bleeding can result.

African Gray Parrots are not given to excessive growth of the beak, which can inhibit the intake of food.But if it does occur, a veterinarian experienced with birds should trim the mandibles.

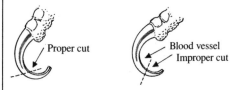

Trimming claws. The drawing on the left shows the correct way; the one on the right, the wrong way. Be careful not to cut into the part that is supplied with blood.

Diseases Relatively Common in African Gray Parrots

Loss of Feathers

We speak of loss of feathers if a bird keeps shedding feathers, preening itself frantically, and pecking constantly at skin and plumage. Eventually the sparse plumage gives way to bald spots, particularly on parts of the head and on the abdomen and the underside of the wings.

Diseases and How to Keep Your Parrot Healthy

Possible causes: Feather mites, lice, and burrowing mites; nutritional deficiencies; metabolic and hormonal imbalances; feather plucking; temperature and humidity changes; etc.

Measures to take: For any of the external parasites, ask the veterinarian or the pet dealer for medication. Remove the bird from its cage and then disinfect all objects the bird comes in contact with, including the cage, the climbing tree, and the entire area where the bird spends its time. But *never* use a spray on the bird itself! Particles of the spray may enter the nose, beak, or eyes and seriously endanger the bird's health. Dust the parrot sparingly with a flea and tick powder containing pyrethin or cabaryl and be careful to cover the bird's nose and eyes while you do it. Since the eggs of mites and lice are not killed by the powder, the procedure has to be repeated after five days, and then again after another seven, and finally after another ten days. If the loss of feathers was not caused by parasites, take the bird to a veterinarian for examination.

Malformed Feathers

Sometimes the new feathers growing in after the molt are so changed in color and shape that your African Gray gradually assumes an entirely new appearance. Often the plumage lacks sheen or is ragged. Flight feathers on wings and tail, as well as smaller feathers, may remain stuck in their sheaths with only a small brush emerging at the upper end of the sticklike body of the feather.

Possible causes: A cage that is too small, insufficient opportunity for exercise, nutritional deficiencies, hormonal imbalances, reduced blood supply after injuries, cysts in the feather follicles.

Measures to take: Give the bird more freedom of movement and check the diet; if the veterinarian can eliminate other possible causes, he will prescribe a tonic to improve general health. Cysts in the feather follicles (a thickening underneath the epidermis) have to be treated by a veterinarian.

Feather Plucking

Unfortunately, African Gray Parrots do succumb to this "bad habit," which can often lead to serious illness and even death. The affected birds keep pecking at their plumage and pull out a significant portion of it. The pain that this causes does not stop them from plucking more, sometimes until they are bloody and finally completely bare.

Possible causes: Different people attribute this disorder to different causes. Many experienced aviculturists and veterinarians think that feather plucking is caused by psychic problems arising from loneliness and boredom, separation from a loved human being or an avian partner, jealousy over a new baby, change of owner, or adjustment to a new home. Others regard it as a manifestation of nutritional deficiencies or allergies. Too small a cage, lack of sleep, insufficient bathing, and too little humidity have also been cited as causes.

Measures to take: Have the bird checked for parasites and for skin disorders and initiate treatment if necessary. Check the diet and add nutritional supplements. Allow the bird to sleep up to 12 hours in a darkened room. Eliminate negative influences, such as loud noises and optical irritations; and, if the bird

43

has been neglected, spend more time with it. Offer lots of fresh branches for gnawing on. Spray the bird frequently with Bitter Apple (available at pet stores), lukewarm water, or set up a bath. Dab olive oil on the bald spots. Putting an "Elizabethan" collar on the bird (which only a veterinarian should do) to prevent feather plucking is likely to aggravate the psychic maladies that are often the cause of the problem. If no one in the family has time to devote to the bird several times a day, it may be best to find a second bird to keep the first one company.

This bird is a victim of feather plucking. The prime causes are loneliness, boredom, and lack of sufficient exercise.

Symptoms that May Indicate Serious Illness

Shortness of Breath, Noisy Breathing

Apathy, lack of appetite, and a discharge from the nostrils often accompany shortness of breath. The bird obviously has more difficulty than usual breathing and inhales through the bill; in serious cases you can also hear rattling, pumping, or wheezing sounds.

Possible causes: Unfortunately these symptoms accompany all kinds of diseases, and only a veterinarian will be able to arrive at an exact diagnosis.

Measures to take: Keep the bird quiet and use a heat lamp to provide even warmth (about 86° F [30° C] day and night). Substitute weak black or camomile tea — lukewarm — for the water, and offer soft food made of low-fat cottage cheese, hard-boiled egg, and zwieback softened in water. The veterinarian will prescribe further treatment.

Throwing up Slime

Parrots occasionally throw up out of nervousness, great fear, or sudden fright. Male parrots, when they are in a breeding mood, sometimes also choke up seeds together with some slimy juices from their crop in an attempt to feed a human partner they are attached to. But if a parrot keeps throwing up partially digested seeds mixed with a sticky, stringy, brown substance from the crop, you have to assume that it is seriously ill. This symptom is often accompanied by shortness of breath, noisy breathing, and diarrhea.

Possible cause: Crop inflammation.

Measures to take: Remove food; substitute camomile tea for the drinking water; take the parrot to the veterinarian as soon as you can.

Diarrhea

A healthy African Gray Parrot produces droppings about every forty minutes. Normal excreta have a definite shape: They consist

44

Diseases and How to Keep Your Parrot Healthy

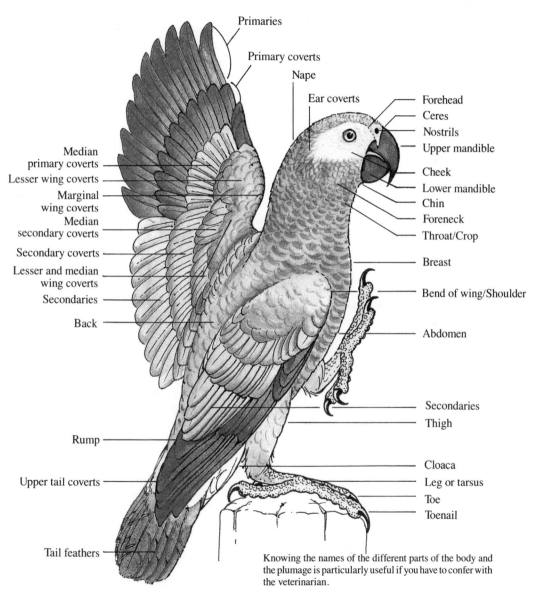

Knowing the names of the different parts of the body and the plumage is particularly useful if you have to confer with the veterinarian.

Diseases and How to Keep Your Parrot Healthy

of a white dab of semisolid urine on a rim of dark stool. But a nervous parrot responds to anything frightening or exciting by extruding excreta, which then may be mushy or sometimes almost liquid. If the frequency and the consistency of the droppings gradually return to normal and if the bird appears well and lively, there is nothing to worry about. But if the droppings remain soft to runny, you should have the bird examined even if its behavior is otherwise normal.

If there is any obvious change in a parrot's excreta; if the change lasts for several days and the droppings are not only watery but slimy, fermenting, discolored, or mixed with blood; and if the bird seems weak or sick, visit the veterinarian as quickly as possible. A lab analysis of a stool sample is essential. **Possible causes**: Most illnesses an African Gray Parrot is likely to succumb to are accompanied by more or less serious diarrhea. If the analysis of a stool sample reveals no parasites or bacterial or mycological pathogens, the problem may be caused by one of the following: a cold (because of drafts, a cool bath, or sudden drop in temperature); not enough grit (see page 36); poisoning (see List of Dangers, page 31); wrong or spoiled food. If none of these apply, the bird may be suffering from a kidney or liver problem, an infectious disease, or from tumors, none of which show up in the droppings. **Measures to take**: In the case of colds (which usually manifest themselves in a discharge from the nostrils) use a heat lamp on the bird (see page 41); sprinkle some medicinal charcoal over the birdseed; replace the drinking water with camomile tea (make sure there is always a ready supply); temporarily stop feeding fruit and greens. Offer

bread with peanut butter, cooked oatmeal, and vegetable baby food with some Kaopectate (15 drops per ounce of water). The result should be a solid stool. Alternatively, you might try the cooled water of boiled rice. If there is not enough grit, see page 36. At the slightest suspicion of poisoning, call your veterinarian instantly (on weekends or holidays, call whomever is on emergency duty). Only a veterinarian can tell you what measures are called for.

Psittacosis (also called ornithosis)

Psittacosis affects not only parrots but other birds and humans as well. When other birds have the disease, it is called ornithosis. Psittacosis, like many other diseases affecting parrots, has no unique symptoms that make it easy to recognize. But a parrot suffering from psittacosis hardly ever eats, and the disease is often accompanied by diarrhea, crop inflammation, severe breathing difficulties, discharge from the nose, enteritis, and conjunctivitis with a pussy discharge. In severe cases the bird may even have cramps or be paralyzed. If humans are infected, the first symptoms resemble those of the flu but then develop into something like pneumonia. Psittacosis is far from harmless for humans, and medical attention is essential at the slightest suspicion. **Possible activators**: Unhygienic conditions, poor diet, lack of fresh air and exercise, changes from one place to another, transport,

Above: African Gray Parrot chicks about 35 days old. Below: An African Gray Parrot taking a walk in a meadow.

Diseases and How to Keep Your Parrot Healthy

weakened state after a basically harmless sickness or after molting, or psychic unhappiness caused by loneliness, the death of a partner, or neglect by the keeper can all contribute to an active outbreak of psittacosis. Sometimes African Gray Parrots that have been kept in a cage for years suddenly develop psittacosis because they have been carrying the pathogen (chlamydia) in latent form all along. Birds living in an aviary may catch the disease from infected wild birds. In that case, danger of contagion exists for both birds and humans.

Measures to take: The pathogen can be detected in the excreta, and if the symptoms described above occur, a stool sample should be analyzed promptly. The disease has to be reported to public-health officials, who will determine where and how the bird is to be treated.

The Trip to the Veterinarian

When you take your parrot to the veterinarian you have to protect it from drafts and, depending on the situation, from cold, wetness, and wind (wrap the cage in a blanket). Cover the bottom tray with a paper cage liner that is lightly "waxed" on one side (which prevents moisture from leaking through to the tray) because the veterinarian should have a stool sample free of sand for examination.

Jacob's favorite perch is a shelf in the kitchen cupboards. Above: Jacob opens the door without anyone's help and climbs onto a pot in the cupboard. Below, left: This is how he closes the door after himself. Below, right: In this position he contemplates the world and his own thoughts.

You will be able to facilitate the veterinarian's diagnosis if you can answer the following questions: How old is the bird? From what pet store (or what breeder) did you buy it and how long have you had it? Did it have previous owners? How long has it looked sickly? What changes in its behavior and routine have you observed? Has the bird been sick before? What was the illness then, and how was it treated? Do you have other pets? Are all members of the family (including other pets) healthy?

Be sure to take along a sample of the birdseed mixture that has made up the bulk of the parrot's diet for the last few weeks. List the additional foods the bird gets and mention anything unusual it might have eaten in the last few days.

This way the veterinarian can get a picture of the situation quickly and point out any mistakes of care there might be. A bacteriological and parasitological analysis of the stool is also essential. If this does not reveal the cause of illness, ask if there are other diagnostic procedures, such as X-rays or biopsies. Make sure you understand what is involved in any suggested procedure. Ask if it is really necessary, what the chances of success are, and what would happen if you refuse to give your consent. If your veterinarian recommends a medical treatment, follow his directions conscientiously, giving the prescribed medication in the correct amount, at the correct times, and for the required length of time. Trying to experiment would be irresponsible. Also ask if there is anything else you can do to speed up recovery, such as changes in diet and environment or use of a heat lamp.

Diseases and How to Keep Your Parrot Healthy

Giving Medication

If medication is added to the drinking water — by far the best method — you must make sure the bird has no other source of liquids. Remove bath water, keep the bird away from dripping faucets, and feed no fruit or vegetables. If the medication is sprinkled or dribbled over the birdseed, don't fill the dish because a clever parrot will toss out the top layer of seeds with the unaccustomed taste with its bill and get the seed below. If the medication has to be introduced into the beak, hold your tame parrot gently under your left arm (between your elbow and body) and hold its head from behind with your left hand without pressing against its larynx. A parrot that is not tame may bite out of fear and has to be handled by two people. Wrap the bird in a thick towel; then ask your assistant to hold it with both arms against the chest, holding the head steady from behind with one hand to keep the parrot from biting and dodging. The bird should be in a sitting position, not flat on its back! Liquid medicine should be dripped on the tongue from the side to keep it from getting into the trachea and choking the bird.

Understanding African Gray Parrots

Many African Gray Parrots talk, and some master a surprisingly large number of amusing word combinations, but only very few learn to produce expressions and short sentences in the appropriate context. Only the brightest among them say "Good morning" exclusively in the morning and "Good night" only in the evening. Most of them spout these greetings indiscriminately and only by coincidence at the appropriate occasion. But it is not the words of human speech your African Gray has learned to imitate that will help you understand your pet; its own highly differentiated forms of expression, the bird's innate vocal and body language, its typical patterns of behavior are the real keys to its nature.

Distribution and Appearance

The African Gray Parrot's area of distribution lies in western Africa between 17 degrees west and 32 degrees east longitude and 10 degrees north and 10 degrees south latitude (see map of distribution, page 51). The African Gray Parrot, sometimes also called Yaco, is part of the Parrot family, whose scientific name is Psittacidae. Within this family the African Gray belongs to the tribe of Psittacini, or Blunt-tailed Parrots, which in turn forms part of the subfamily Psittacinae, or True Parrots. There is only one species of African Gray Parrot: *Psittacus erithacus Linne 1758*. Some ornithologists regard the Timneh Parrot (*P. e. timneh Fraser 1844*), which differs somewhat from the nominate form *P. e. erithacus*, as a true subspecies; others see it merely as a variant or race. The Timneh Parrot, which occurs in Liberia,

African Gray Parrots come from Africa. Their area of distribution includes the following countries: Ivory Coast, Ghana, Togo, Benin, Nigeria, Chad, Cameroon, Central African Republic, Zaire, Uganda, Kenya, Burundi, Tanzania, Angola, Congo Republic, Gabon, Equatorial Guinea, and the islands Principe and Fernando Po.

the westernmost parts of the Ivory Coast, and in Sierra Leone, differs from the nominate African Gray Parrot in size (it is clearly smaller), in its maroon tail, and in the beige to pink color of the upper third of the upper mandible.

Another subspecies of *P. erithacus*, the Ghana African Gray Parrot (*P. e. princeps Boyd Alexander*), which is darker than the nominate form, is restricted to the islands of Principe and Fernando Po in the Gulf of Guinea. Differences in size and weight often account for the highly divergent data found in the literature on African Gray Parrots. Thus the weight is given as anywhere from 8 to 19.5 ounces (230–550 g); overall length, from 13 to 16 inches (32–41 cm); and length of wing, from 8 3/4 to 9 3/4 inches (22–24.5 cm).

Understanding African Gray Parrots

Like many other kinds of birds, African Gray Parrots show some variations in color. Some individuals are darker than others, and the light margins on the breast feathers vary from almost invisible to quite prominent. There are also a few reports of African Gray Parrots with red wing coverts, red thighs, and red feathers on the abdomen.These so-called king birds represent deviations, not a separate race. In addition, there are instances of pet birds that grow red feathers on the breast and/or back for no known reason after a molt or a sickness (see color photos on page 48).

African Gray Parrots Living in the Wild

Unfortunately we don't have much detailed information about how African Gray Parrots live in their native Africa. People familiar with the areas inhabited by African Grays report that the birds live primarily in forested hill country up to an altitude of about 4,000 feet (1,200 m). They favor mangrove woods where they climb and fly around in the tall trees in search of food. They form flocks and fly swiftly along set routes to watering places. When darkness falls, they return to their accustomed sleeping places high above the ground. Their favorite foods are various kinds of fruit found in the forest, nuts, berries, and the fruit of oil palms. It is not altogether clear whether or not they also consume insect eggs and larvae or other forms of animal protein. But they are frequently observed feeding on half-ripe corn in cultivated fields.

Mating and Incubation

African Grays live in flocks of one to two hundred birds, and when they reach sexual maturity they enter a lifelong, monogamous sexual bond. They are in no hurry to settle down and will accept only a mate they feel drawn to. For the mating season, each pair retreats to its nest hole, usually in a decaying tree. Knotholes and hollows in tree trunks are expanded with the beak and made deeper, so that the nest cavity, which is carpeted with pulpy wood fragments, is about 20 inches (50 cm) below the entry hole. The nest holes are hidden from view in the foliage of the trees, but the flock sticks close together, finding nests in trees in the same vicinity, so that contact is maintained during the breeding season. Since African Gray Parrots are distributed over a large area with varying weather conditions, it is not entirely clear whether climatic conditions are the sole factor responsible for the timing of the mating period or whether other influences are at work, too. When the birds come into breeding condition, the male feeds his mate, and both birds sing soft, monotonous notes.The female soon starts sleeping in the nest cavity while the male guards the nest or sleeps next to the entry hole. The female then lays three to five eggs at intervals of two to three days. The eggs are roundish to oval and weigh 19 to 22 grams. Once the hen has settled on the eggs to incubate them, she is fed entirely by the male, who barely eats at all during this period. The female leaves the nest only in the morning and evening to deposit droppings.

Rearing of the Young and Their Development

Incubation lasts 30 days. After that, the

Understanding African Gray Parrots

Mutual preening. African Gray Parrots spend a lot of time preening each other's plumage, especially in the spots that a bird cannot reach with its own beak.

male continues to bring food, now for both the female and the nestlings. By the time the chicks are about 10 weeks old their plumage is almost completely grown in. When they emerge from the nest hole at 12 weeks, they first practice climbing and are still fed — now by both parents. They still have to learn to find soft food for themselves and to eat it. The upper mandible of young African Grays does not take on its characteristic curve and hardness until the birds are three to four months old, and it is only then that they can begin to eat fruits with hard shells. From the fifth to the eighth month, the ash-gray eyes gradually take on the light yellow color characteristic of mature birds. During this period, too, the faint red on the tail feathers turns bright red, and the young birds gradually develop into self-confident flyers. But until the first molt, which occurs at about one year, the plumage remains mottled brown

and somewhat darker than that of the parents. However, the young birds become independent and take their place as regular members in the life of the flock before this.

Vocal Expressions

The speech of a young African Gray that has been caught in the wild is at first purely "African." Loud jungle screeches at all levels of pitch are the vocal expression of fear and terror, of the desire for contact with other parrots, and, after a while, of the joy at being alive and even of feeling at ease. These sounds have a primeval quality and are impressive, but they are foreign and incomprehensible to our ears. The quicker an African Gray adjusts to its new surroundings and the less it is left by itself, the sooner the loud screeching will subside.

Mimicking: A communicative bird will try to impress the feared or respected creatures around it — that is, the humans — by imitating the sounds of their world with its voice. As a born vocal mimic, it will react enthusiastically to whistling and will quickly learn to imitate short tunes in all kinds of keys and degrees of loudness. This can lead to lively exchanges and to impressive repertoires of melodies. I know African Gray Parrots that can whistle "Lightly Row," the "Radetzky March," and the so-called "Duck Dance"; one even whistles *Der Vogelfänger bin ich ja* from the *Magic Flute*. I have already mentioned that many African Grays imitate words and short sentences they hear from their human family. The real geniuses among them may master several hundred words; less gifted ones never learn more than a few expressions and prefer whistling.

Innate utterances: If you want to get a sense of your parrot's moods, you should listen to the sounds that hark back to its own innate "language." Since African Grays are individualists, there are no general rules about what certain sounds mean. You have to listen to your particular bird and learn to interpret its utterances. When an African Gray is terrified, it usually falls silent. But if it tries to discourage a feared creature or object from approaching closer, it may growl loudly or spit. You may also hear a soft spitting or growling when the parrot is trying to feed its favorite person or when it is enjoying being scratched. If someone it is fond of leaves the room, it may protest with a short, high-pitched squealing sound, and it may also squeal softly and briefly several times in succession as an invitation to play or as a request for affection. When it comes up to a person, you can sometimes hear a soft "Nh, nh" or a quiet clicking of the tongue. Of course African Gray Parrots also intermingle parts of their own speech with sounds they have learned to imitate and with whistling and babbling. And whenever your African Gray is resting quietly and peacefully you will hear the sounds of a relaxed whetting and grinding of the bill.

Physical Agility

Flying: To cover larger distances, African Gray Parrots fly fast and straight. The flock flies together just above the tree tops in a direct line to wherever it is headed.

Climbing: In the dense branches of trees, climbing is a sensible method of locomotion, and it is typical of African Grays. Their feet are ideally adapted for climbing, with the two middle toes pointing forward and the other two backward. But the bill also plays an important role. When moving from one branch to another, the parrot first reaches for the new perch with its bill, the body forming a taut, horizontal bridge. Then one foot moves forward, forcing the legs to splay as in a dancer's split. Finally, when the first foot has found a secure hold, the second leg is pulled to the new branch. African Grays can move on a vertical surface both head up and head down. When moving downward, the parrot supports its weight with muscular neck and uses its beak like a brake shoe. The birds also like to hang head down by one or both legs while they look around for the next good hold. Even minute cracks and bits of branches offer enough of a hold for the beak. If there is nothing to get a hold of when climbing up a smooth tree trunk, a parrot will raise itself to its full height, reach for the next higher branch with the beak, and swing both legs up. If you have a sturdy climbing tree with strong, natural branches that are securely mounted, these daredevil climbers will never come to harm. But the parrot's overwhelming need for climbing can be dangerous if, instead of natural branches, smooth, round dowels have been used in the climbing tree, especially if they turn, are loose, or might fall out of their holes. If there is such a mishap, the parrot may be able to fly or flutter on its way down and land gently — assuming that the tree is far enough above the ground and the wings have not been clipped.

Walking: An African Gray Parrot walking across an even surface looks clumsy and funny because its large, prehensile feet are

Understanding African Gray Parrots

somewhat pigeon-toed. The bird has to proceed cautiously in order not to trip over its own feet. But if you see the same animal move in a tree, you'll see immediately that this is the kind of locomotion the feet are adapted to. When the parrot moves sideways on a branch, the inward turn of the feet helps one foot move across the other and take a firm hold, first with one foot and then with the other.

Like all other large parrots, African Grays also use their toes to reach for and hold onto things. Thus they pick up fruit, cookies, bread, and nuts with their toes and eat them the way we do (see drawing on page 8).

Flying "in place." African Gray Parrots that are unable to fly exercise their flight muscles by beating their wings vigorously. Usually they hold on to a branch or the cage wall with their beak while doing this.

Moods

For all birds that live in social communities the way African Gray Parrots do, moods play an important part in the cohesion of the group. Certain sounds and movements create the same mood in the entire flock, so that all the members feel like resting, preening themselves, taking to the air, or entering the mating cycle at the same time. No bird stays behind at a watering place, for instance, when the rest of the flock returns to the nesting trees. If it did, it would expose itself to much greater danger than when it is surrounded by the flock. When all the pairs get ready to mate, all the available nest holes in the birds' territory are occupied; all the males watch out more alertly for danger; and the entire social life of the birds adapts itself to the needs of the developing young.

How to Recognize the Moods of Your Parrot

An African Gray Parrot that is kept singly and misses the influence of others of its kind expresses its moods spontaneously and is confused and upset when its human companion misunderstands its signals or interferes with its routines. The keeper should therefore get acquainted with some of his parrot's body language to be able to interpret it and respond to it correctly.

Fear: When a bird is relaxed and not nervous about anything, its plumage hugs its body loosely. But when something frightening happens, the feathers are flattened tightly to the body as the bird tries to make itself look as thin as possible, stretches its head high, and stares at one spot with narrowed pupils. When the bird relaxes because the moment of

55

fear is past, a decision has been made, or some exciting action is over, the feathers are raised all of a sudden and shaken. The old mood gives way instantly to a new one. Sometimes the bird shakes only the tail feathers to indicate a change of mood.

Ease and readiness for contact: When a parrot is relaxed, it often sits in rest position on one leg with the feathers, particularly those of the chest and abdomen, loosely fluffed up. Sometimes the abdominal feathers vibrate slightly. This may look as though the bird were trembling with fear, but it is more a sign of slight insecurity or a desire for affection. If the bird is truly content and at ease, not only the belly feathers are fluffed up; the feathers on the chin, throat, ears, and cheeks also stand up to form a ruff, and you can often hear a soft grinding of the bill. It is these feathers and those of the nape that are the main key to an African Gray Parrot's good moods, such as relaxation, a feeling of well-being, and receptivity to contact. The desire for contact is expressed even more explicitly when the parrot lowers its head way down with raised feathers as an invitation to being scratched. African Grays are also completely relaxed when they preen themselves. The feathers lie loosely on top of each other so that each is accessible to the bill.

Parrots often stretch after having spent some time in one position. Each leg extends backward, one at a time; the toes curl in a loose fist; and the wing of that side is raised slightly and moved backward. Raising both wings straight up and stretching them is part of the same routine. But this motion is also used to regulate temperature. If a bird is too warm, it raises both wings to get cooler.

Flying mood: An African Gray Parrot that cannot fly because its living space is too confined or because its wings are clipped still has to exercise its flight muscles several times a day. During these vigorous movements it is not enough for the bird to hold on to a perch or branch or the cage wall with its feet; the bill also has to be able to grab on to something securely. This shows what power the parrot would expend if it were actually flying, something it has learned by bitter experience it cannot do in its confined quarters. When an African Gray is in one of these flying moods, the wing flapping is often accompanied by calls which in the wild would surely act as a stimulus for the whole flock to take to the air.

Intelligence and Disposition

African Gray Parrots have long had a reputation for being smart, and we may indeed assume that the species has considerable native intelligence. But in parrots, as in all creatures, individual development and environmental factors also play an important role, and there are vast differences between individuals in the level of innate intelligence. For an animal, and especially for a bird like the African Gray Parrot, intelligence means the ability to apply innate behavior and mechanisms of reaction — instincts, in other words — in new situations and modify them for a desired purpose. The life of a captive African Gray offers plenty of illustrations: A parrot sits in its locked cage and would like to get out. It knows from experience where the door is and that if the door were not locked there would be a way to freedom.

Understanding African Gray Parrots

Nobody knows what is going on in the parrot's head as it stares at the door. But when it proceeds to tinker on the lock with its beak, it is clear that the strength and skills of the beak are being put to use in an — often successful — attempt to spring the lock.

Intelligence is also at work when a parrot produces certain sounds or words in a context where they make sense. There are African Gray Parrots that keep saying "Good night" in the evening until the light is turned off and the cage is covered because they want the room to be quiet so that they can go to sleep.

African Grays also have amazing memories. For many years I had an African Gray Parrot as a summer guest. Every year before the bird arrived I would sprout some seeds because ordinarily it did not get this healthy treat. I always offered the sprouts at the same spot. The parrot soon acquired a taste for this delicacy and from then on waited for me every morning in that exact spot. Each summer, on the very first day, the bird greeted me there, waiting for sprouts even though the rest of the year it never tasted sprouted seeds.

The intelligence of birds has been objectively rated by the ethologist Otto Koehler, who devised a scientific experiment involving the picking up of seeds one by one to test how high different birds can count. According to Koehler, budgerigars and jackdaws can count to six; pigeons only get to five, whereas common crows, magpies, Yellow-fronted Amazons, and African Gray Parrots count up to seven.

Mistrust and Fear: Hardly any other parrot is as well endowed with these qualities as the African Gray. But no matter how frightened and suspicious a newly acquired African Gray Parrot may be, it will, from the safe vantage point of its cage, keep a very sharp eye on its surroundings and on everything that is going on. Before long it learns to accept things that happen regularly. It also gets used to noises that occur often and stops worrying about them. But the living creatures around it are the primary focus of the bird's scrutiny; it observes with minute attention how they move, what objects they handle, and — above all — how they relate to it. Eventually the parrot classifies everyone it sees and everything that happens around it as either "unpleasant and possibly dangerous" or as "normal and harmless."

Every unfamiliar item, no matter how small and insignificant, is at first assigned to the first category. Thus the first sight of a peanut may elicit a terrified response. If the peanut is in the food dish, the African Gray will cautiously and with craned neck peck out a few seeds from the dish, making sure not to touch the suspicious foreign object. After a few days the bird may muster enough courage to dispose of the peanut with a hurried toss of the bill. Now a few more peanuts should be put in the cage outside the dish. The parrot will try to whisk the offending things out of sight again and again, until one day — in the case I am describing this took seven months — curiosity wins out over suspicion and the bird begins to nibble on the peanut. In this process the kernels are at first ignored and only the shell is investigated with the bill. Eventually, by sheer chance, a kernel is picked up and tasted, and now the parrot quickly learns what the peanut is for and how to deal with it. Overcoming this degree of suspiciousness obviously takes a lot of time, and an African Gray will never be entirely free of mistrust. An African Gray claims its territory only bit by bit and is able to acknowledge and accept pleasant things only slowly. And there may be relapses at any point: People it has begun to trust may throw the bird into a panic if they appear with a striking hat, or if they lower the Venetian blinds unexpectedly or merely change the angle of the slats, or if they set up an ironing board close to the cage for the first time.

Partnership between Bird and Human

An African Gray that is kept singly as a pet has to find a surrogate partner to have an outlet for all its innate social needs. To simply give it a mirror would be pointless. An African Gray Parrot is not duped so easily; it needs an intelligent response to its gestures of communication.

Scratching: Usually the first body contact between bird and human takes the form of scratching the head. No matter how shy a bird may be, at some point it will lower its head and raise the feathers on the nape slightly as an invitation to be scratched. Watch your parrot closely; it is the bird that determines just where and how much it wants to be scratched. If the head is lowered without the feathers fluffed up this means that you should not scratch against the lie of the feathers. A slight fluffing up shows which spot on the head or nape may be petted with the fingers between two rows of feathers. Eventually the bird will enjoy it if you pet one row after the other. But before you get to

that point, you and your bird have to gradually build up mutual trust. Quite often the parrot will suddenly shrink away from your hand, turn its head, and try to hack at your finger. This is no sign of malice. An inexperienced bird partner engaged in mutual preening would receive the same treatment. Sometimes feathers that are just growing in and are still wrapped in their delicate sheaths are touched wrong during the scratching. This makes the bird flinch and scratch the spot with its own toes and perhaps hack at you. If you react by yanking your hand back suddenly to get away from the beak, this will shake the bird's confidence. Try to respond as calmly as you can and talk to the bird soothingly. If the bird does strike you, don't scream "Ouch!" because the parrot would take this as a sign that it has won out and then try to assert its superiority again and again. You would not even have to scream anymore; the parrot would do it for you.

Playful contact: Quite often the scratching of the head suddenly turns into a playful tussle. If you keep a careful eye on your parrot you will notice by the rapid changes in the bird's pupils that the enjoyment is no longer unmixed. Without any apparent reason, the beak is raised for a strike, though obviously not with the intent of hitting you. If you now wave your hand up and down in front of the beak, the bird will follow your movements with obvious delight, bowing rapidly. If you touch the beak lightly from above, the game speeds up. You can change the motion so that the parrot's head and neck follow your hand in elegant figure-eight

Understanding African Gray Parrots

This touching gesture can sometimes be observed when the bird's favorite person leaves the room. In its agitation the parrot raises its foot to its bill and seems to chew its nails.

sweeps. African Grays seem to engage in this type of horse play with great pleasure. But watch out: If the bird nabs your hand, it will bite with full force — again, not out of meanness but because a real partner would be protected by a layer of thick feathers.

It is quite easy to terminate these wild sessions by simply rubbing one's fingernail against a branch or perch or the edge of a table, thus imitating the sound of a parrot whetting its bill. A parrot always whets its bill after eating, no matter how small the snack, but cleaning is not the only purpose of the gesture; it also has a function in maintaining peaceful contact with the partner. If you rub your fingernails together, your parrot will immediately follow suit by whetting its bill as close to your hand as possible. If

you also touch its upper mandible or gently run two fingers along its bill, you will evoke an affectionate mood. An African Gray that feels close to you will then try to feed you. With a snakelike movement of the neck, it regurgitates some food from the crop, tries to get hold of one of your fingers with one foot, and deposits the food in your hand. Sometimes a parrot will investigate your face, trying to find the appropriate place for the food. My African Gray, Moses, used to plaster the softened grains onto my nose or behind my ear. But usually he takes a gentle hold of my finger with his bill and deposits his gift there. If this ceremony is accompanied by a soft hissing sound, this is a sign that your parrot feels great tenderness for you.

"Courtship and Hostile Display": The great German ethologist Heinroth coined this phrase for all animal behavior that serves both to intimidate and to woo. Parrots are monogamous and woo their mates not only at the onset of the mating season but express mutual affection at other times as well. However, threatening gestures are also part of flock life. Thus, this kind of display is an integral part of an African Gray's behavior, and it is not surprising that it also turns up in captive birds. African Gray Parrots, unlike many other birds, rarely perform these instinctive acts as meaningless routines. After all, they are among the most intelligent of birds, and they need a partner to make the full extent of the interplay possible. If an African Gray has formed a special bond with a member of its human family, it will pick that person to demonstrate its affections in wooing as well as intimidating actions. Feeding the chosen person partially digested seeds choked up from the crop is such a proof of love, as are gentle nibbling on hands and earlobes, careful cleaning of the cheeks, or the unmistakable request for attention which is expressed by the bill's repeated knocking against an object.

Respond to your African Gray's offers of affection as often and with as much enthusiasm as possible! This is the only way you can even partially make up for the absence of natural partners.

Partner feeding. During the courtship and mating period the male feeds the female. Partner feeding at other times serves to strengthen the bond between the pair.

Useful Publications and Addresses

Books

Diemer, Petra. *Parrots*. Woodbury, N.Y.:
  Barron's Educational Series, Inc., 1983.
Forshaw, J. M. *Parrots of the World*. 2nd
  ed. Melbourne: Landsdowne Press, 1978.
Lantermann, Werner. *New Parrot Handbook*.
  Woodbury, N.Y.: Barron's Educational
  Series, Inc., 1986.
Low, Rosemary. *Parrots, Their Care and
  Breeding*. 2nd ed. Poole and Dorset, Eng-
  land: Blandford Press, 1986.
Rutgers, A., and Norris, K. A. *Encyclopedia
  of Aviculture*, Vol. II. Poole and Dorset,
  England: Blandford Press, 1970.
Vriends, Matthew. *Simon and Schuster's
  Guide to Pet Birds*. New York: Simon and
  Schuster, 1984.

Magazines

American Cage Bird Magazine, Inc.
One Glamore Court
Smithtown, NY 11787

Bird Talk
P. O. Box 3940
San Clemente, CA 92672

Societies

American Federation of Aviculture
2208 ''A'' Artesia Boulevard
Redondo Beach, CA 90278
(Publishes the bi-monthly *The A. F. A.
  Watchbird*, undoubtedly the best avicul-
  tural magazine around)

National Parrot Association
8 North Hoffman Lane
Hauppauge, NY 11788
(Publishes a bi-monthly journal)

Society of Parrot Breeders and Exhibitors
c/o Dr. A. Decoteau
Groton Street
Dunstable, MA 01827

The Avicultural Society of America, Inc.
P. O. Box 157
Stanton, CA 90680
(Publishes a monthly bulletin)

The Association of Avian Veterinarians
P.O. Box 299
East Northport, NY 11731
(Tel. 516/757-6320)

Index

Index

Perfect for Pet Owners!

PET OWNER'S MANUALS

Over 50 illustrations per book (20 or more color photos), 72–80 pp., paperback.

AFRICAN GRAY PARROTS (3773-1)
AMAZON PARROTS (4035-X)
BANTAMS (3687-5)
BEAGLES (3829-0)
BEEKEEPING (4089-9)
BOSTON TERRIERS (1696-3)
BOXERS (4036-8)
CANARIES (4611-0)
CATS (4442-8)
CHINCHILLAS (4037-6)
CHOW-CHOWS (3952-1)
CICHLIDS (4597-1)
COCKATIELS (4610-2)
COCKATOOS (4159-3)
CONURES (4880-6)
DACHSHUNDS (1843-5)
DALMATIANS (4605-6)
DISCUS FISH (4669-2)
DOBERMAN PINSCHERS (2999-2)
DOGS (4822-9)
DWARF RABBITS (1352-2)
ENGLISH SPRINGER SPANIELS (1778-1)
FEEDING AND SHELTERING BACKYARD
    BIRDS (4252-2)
FEEDING AND SHELTERING EUROPEAN
    BIRDS (2858-9)
FERRETS (2976-3)
GERBILS (3725-1)
GERMAN SHEPHERDS (2982-8)
GOLDEN RETRIEVERS (3793-6)
GOLDFISH (2975-5)
GOULDIAN FINCHES (4523-8)
GUINEA PIGS (4612-9)
HAMSTERS (4439-8)
IRISH SETTERS (4663-3)
KEESHONDEN (1560-6)
KILLIFISH (4475-4)
LABRADOR RETRIEVERS (3792-8)
LHASA APSOS (3950-5)
LIZARDS IN THE TERRARIUM (3925-4)
LONGHAIRED CATS (2803-1)
LONG-TAILED PARAKEETS (1351-4)
LORIES AND LORIKEETS (1567-3)
LOVEBIRDS (3726-X)

MACAWS (4768-0)
MICE (2921-6)
MINIATURE PIGS (1356-5)
MUTTS (4126-7)
MYNAHS (3688-3)
PARAKEETS (4437-1)
PARROTS (4823-7)
PERSIAN CATS (4405-3)
PIGEONS (4044-9)
POMERANIANS (4670-6)
PONIES (2856-2)
POODLES (2812-0)
RABBITS (4440-1)
RATS (4535-1)
ROTTWEILERS (4483-5)
SCHNAUZERS (3949-1)
SHAR-PEI (4334-2)
SHEEP (4091-0)
SHETLAND SHEEPDOGS (4264-6)
SHIH TZUS (4524-6)
SIAMESE CATS (4764-8)
SIBERIAN HUSKIES (4265-4)
SNAKES (2813-9)
SPANIELS (2424-9)
TROPICAL FISH (4700-1)
TURTLES (4702-8)
YORKSHIRE TERRIERS (4406-1)
ZEBRA FINCHES (3497-X)

NEW PET HANDBOOKS

Detailed, illustrated profiles (40–60 color photos), 144 pp., paperback.

NEW AQUARIUM FISH HANDBOOK
    (3682-4)
NEW AUSTRALIAN PARAKEET
    HANDBOOK (4739-7)
NEW BIRD HANDBOOK (4157-7)
NEW CANARY HANDBOOK (4879-2)
NEW CAT HANDBOOK (2922-4)
NEW COCKATIEL HANDBOOK (4201-8)
NEW DOG HANDBOOK (2857-0)
NEW DUCK HANDBOOK (4088-0)
NEW FINCH HANDBOOK (2859-7)
NEW GOAT HANDBOOK (4090-2)
NEW PARAKEET HANDBOOK (2985-2)
NEW PARROT HANDBOOK (3729-4)
NEW RABBIT HANDBOOK (4202-6)

NEW SALTWATER AQUARIUM
    HANDBOOK (4482-7)
NEW SOFTBILL HANDBOOK (4075-9)
NEW TERRIER HANDBOOK (3951-3)

REFERENCE BOOKS

Comprehensive, lavishly illustrated references (60–300 color photos), 136–176 pp., hardcover & paperback.

AQUARIUM FISH (1350-6)
AQUARIUM FISH BREEDING (4474-6)
AQUARIUM FISH SURVIVAL MANUAL
    (5686-8)
AQUARIUM PLANTS MANUAL (1687-4)
BEFORE YOU BUY THAT PUPPY (1750-1)
BEST PET NAME BOOK EVER, THE
    (4258-1)
CARING FOR YOUR SICK CAT (1726-9)
CAT CARE MANUAL (5765-1)
CIVILIZING YOUR PUPPY (4953-5)
COMMUNICATING WITH YOUR DOG
    (4203-4)
COMPLETE BOOK OF BUDGERIGARS
    (6059-8)
COMPLETE BOOK OF CAT CARE (4613-7)
COMPLETE BOOK OF DOG CARE (4158-5)
COMPLETE BOOK OF PARROTS (5971-9)
DOG CARE MANUAL (5764-3)
FEEDING YOUR PET BIRD (1521-3)
GOLDFISH AND ORNAMENTAL CARP
    (5634-5)
GUIDE TO A WELL BEHAVED CAT
    (1476-6)
GUIDE TO HOME PET GROOMING
    (4298-0)
HEALTHY DOG, HAPPY DOG (1842-7)
HOP TO IT: A Guide to Training Your Pet
    Rabbit (4551-3)
HORSE CARE MANUAL (5795-3)
HOW TO TALK TO YOUR CAT (1749-8)
HOW TO TEACH YOUR OLD DOG
    NEW TRICKS (4544-0)
LABYRINTH FISH (5635-3)
MACAWS (6073-3)
NONVENOMOUS SNAKES (5632-9)
WATER PLANTS IN THE AQUARIUM
    (3926-2)

Barron's Educational Series, Inc. • 250 Wireless Blvd., Hauppauge, NY 11788
Call toll-free: 1-800-645-3476 • In Canada: Georgetown Book Warehouse
34 Armstrong Ave., Georgetown, Ont. L7G 4R9 • Call toll-free: 1-800-247-7160
ISBN prefix: 0-8120 • Order from your favorite book or pet store

R 2/94